You Want WHAT?

C000071068

Copyright © 2011 by Mariann Mohos

All rights reserved. No part of this publication may be reproduced, or transmitted in any form or by any means, electronic or mechanical, including photocopying, recording, or by any information storage and retrieval system, without written permission from the author, except for the inclusion of brief quotations in a review.

Cover design by John Kasperowicz and Annie Manning

Book design and text composition by HERIBERT C BT., www.heribertc.hu

ISBN-10   0-9832366-6-6
ISBN-13   9780983236665

Library of Congress Control Number: 2011900026

Printed in the United States

YOU WANT WHAT???

Concierge Tales from the Men and Women
Who Make Las Vegas Dreams Come True

Mariann Mohos

Contents

Chapter 1: Not Quite Rolling a 7 or 11 – Goofy Moments

Chapter 2: Propositions – Unusual Requests

Chapter 3: Odd Numbers Only – Very Unusual Requests

Chapter 4: Ante Up – Money Matters

Chapter 5: Gambling on Love – Love and Marriage

Chapter 6: Stacking the Chips – It's Their Party

Chapter 7: Winning the Pot – Heartfelt Moments

Chapter 8: Paying the Runner – Famous Faces

Chapter 9: What are the Odds? – Funny: Ha Ha!

Chapter 10: BUST! – Funny: Peculiar

Chapter 11: Serious Steam – Naughty Bits

Chapter 12: Counting Their Cards
- Crimes and Misdemeanors

Chapter 13: Longshots – A Time for Miracles

Chapter 14: Appendix

You Want WHAT???

Acknowledgements

I would like to personally thank the following people, who have, in no small way, made a difference in my life, career, and in the writing of this book. To the concierges who gave their stories for this book, not only did you provide the essence of this collection, you have also reminded me over and over again why I love this business.

Zaida Banegas, you are truly the epitome of the perfect concierge. Your positive attitude, kindness, and compassion in the midst of any situation inspire me, and you are the ultimate 'people' person.

John Kasperowicz, there is no way to express how grateful I am for everything you have taught me and the kind of support that you have always given me. With regard to this book especially, you helped make it truly great. Not only professionally, but personally, you have been invaluable. I am eternally grateful to always know that you have my back.

Mike Sikalis, you have been more than a business partner to me. You have been a best friend, a mentor, and someone I deeply respect and admire. I have learned so many valuable things from you, especially that there is a shining opportunity in every challenge and I should never fail to look for it. This, and the other gems of wisdom I have picked up from you, have served me in writing this book and will continue to serve me for the rest of my life. Thank you.

Tom Antion, the amount of respect I have for you is monumental. Your integrity and work ethic is a great inspiration to me, and I would like to take this opportunity to thank you for guiding me through the creation of this book, from planting the first seed to harvesting and enjoying the finished product.

Gerry Culbert, René Vant 'Erve, Ken Stevens, Corinne Cunningham, and Dr. Mitch Mally, your help with this book has truly made it what it is, and I can't thank you enough.

To my friends, Andrea Meszaros, Katalin Pipicz, Eva Paczolay, Nikoletta Kroo, and Anita Babinszki, your input and encouragement has been very valuable, and has helped me make some of the best decisions I've made for this book. I will forever be grateful for your friendship, which has stood the test of time and distance. I have felt your support from Hungary the same as if you have been right beside me all along.

Lajos and Andrea Meszaros at Heribert C Bt, I am so thankful for your time and talent in perfecting this book's layout and overall design. You did such a great job!

To my editors, Samantha Cummings and Richard Horgan, my proofreader, Mirabella Mitchell, Annie Manning, book cover designer, and Aces Graphics, the cartoonists – thank you all for the hard work you've put into the book.

I've saved the very best for last. Thank you to my mother, who taught me from a very early age that every problem comes with a solution. You gave me the ability to skip the panicking and go straight to finding that solution. You also gave me the resilience to stand back up when I fall on my face – and that's something that has served me in this book and in countless other situations.

Thank you to my father. Because of you, I have learned important financial skills that have enabled me to live the kind of life I want, including creating this book. I've been fortunate enough not to struggle the way others have, even when my income wasn't that wonderful. I owe that to you, and I appreciate it very much.

I appreciate each and every one of you, and I hope the resulting product makes you all as proud as you make me.

Introduction

When people ask me what I do for a living and I tell them I'm a concierge, they are immediately intrigued. "Oh, I bet you have some fun stuff going on?!" they exclaim. They become even more intrigued when I tell them the place where I ply my trade – Las Vegas.

Thanks to everything from the 'What happens in Vegas' advertising campaign to movies like *The Hangover,* people have an unending fascination with life on The Strip. They want to know the weirdest question I have ever heard as a Las Vegas concierge, the funniest guest request, the most memorable one, and so on.

Over the years, as I have shared stories about my career as a concierge, people would always want to hear more. This gave me the idea to go out and ask my fellow concierges about their stories, and to compile everything into a book to share it with the world.

I interviewed more than three dozen colleagues from both big and small hotels. Since a cornerstone of our profession is privacy, all guest names have been changed. A few stories have also been modified, at the concierge's request, to further protect the confidentiality of the original parties. But I have taken great care in these instances to make sure the changes did not interfere with the basic narrative.

Interviewing my fellow Las Vegas concierges turned out to be an extremely rewarding experience. Even though most of them would start out the conversation with something along the lines of 'I am sure you've heard it all' or 'No request is too weird,' I soon learned that I definitely had not heard it all and that some requests really should be deemed too strange.

There is truly no limit to the variety of things that happen to a concierge on the Strip. In one conversation, you are talking about where to get the best foie gras, and in the next you are assisting a guest whose quickie marriage has turned out to be the biggest mistake of their young life. Sometimes, we use our network of connections to get things done, while at other moments we are just there to provide a compassionate ear. For the most part though, it's all about helping guests fulfill their personal and vacation dreams.

Finally, I hope that you, the reader, will have as much fun reading through these Las Vegas snippets as I did compiling them. If you happen to have a Las Vegas concierge story of your own that you would like to share, please feel free to email me at the address listed below.

At your service,

Mariann Mohos

July, 2010

lveditors@gmail.com

Not Quite Rolling a 7 or 11

Goofy Moments

People who visit Las Vegas are often star struck by the sights, the sounds, and the amenities. Between this, and the plans that are swirling around in their heads, they sometimes get distracted. Often times, this can lead to silly questions or situations where guests just aren't thinking clearly. Of course, it also leads to a special kind of hilariousness!

Cock-a-Doodle What?

Because wild requests are more often the norm than the exception for Las Vegas concierges, we can sometimes err on the side of the fantastical. A Scottish gentleman who was staying with us called down one morning requesting that we find him a virgin chicken. There's no doubt that we were definitely dubious, but at the same time, determined to please the guest.

Since none of us had ever heard of a virgin chicken, we did the only thing we knew to do and began Googling the term. Needless to say, the search results were off the wall and in some cases, X-rated. Realizing that the Internet wasn't going to get us very far, we began calling a few of the finer restaurants on the Strip, but still, no sign or even knowledge of a so-called virgin chicken.

I was rather embarrassed, because for the most part, Vegas concierges have at least a 'working knowledge' of anything a guest could ask for. We've seen it all and heard it all. So it was with regret that I called the guest and told him that we couldn't find a virgin chicken anywhere. That's when we discovered that the man's thick Scottish accent had been a problem.

He'd asked for a "Virgin check-in," as in Virgin Atlantic Airlines. He jetted back home after some gentle ribbing of the staff member who had taken his first call, and no doubt shared this story with glee back in Glasgow. Who can blame him?

Lost in Translation

Calls from guests who are already in their rooms are fairly routine. The guest might need something picked up or something taken to their rooms. When a call came down once and a guest said, "Can I have a tubastic sent to my room?" it took me a few beats to respond. "I'm sorry, sir," I reply. "What is it that you need?"

"A tubastic," the guest answers. Squinting (as if this might help me translate the word the man was saying), I ask, "Toothpaste?" The guest says, "Yes. Yes." Relieved that I'd figured it out, I tell the guest it will be no problem. "I'll send the toothpaste up with the bellman."

Thinking the dilemma had been solved, I didn't expect it when the man comes down a few minutes later and points to the toothpaste. "No, no, no. A tubastic." He's pointing to his mouth and making an 'in and out movement.' The whole time, I'm thinking, *Oh my gosh! What does he need?*

I said, "Do you need a toothbrush, sir?" He nods. "Yes." So, I present him with a toothbrush, saying, "Here you are, sir." The guest looks at the toothbrush and shakes his head. "No. no. no. I need a tubastic." And again, his mouth opens and he moves his hand in and out.

By this point, I'm beginning to panic because it's clear to me that this man needs something, and I want to give it to him, but for the life of me I don't know what it is that he needs. Suddenly, the movement of his hand changes a little and then the little light bulb above my head goes off. I say, "Oh! You need a toothpick."

"Yes! Yes! Yes."

Silly Questions

Not long ago, a guest asked my colleague how to spell "O." This is a popular show, and it's named O.

Many questions are weather-related, and it's as if the guests think all concierges have built in weather-detectors in their heads. "What time is it going to rain tomorrow?" is one that I've heard quite often, or "When is it going to stop raining?" I've even had a guest ask, "Will it rain in October?" I don't think these questions are filtered before they exit the guests' mouths!

There's one particular man who was a surgeon, and he was running late for his flight. He calls right down and he says, "Look, get on the phone with the airline. Tell them they're going to have to hold the plane." At first I thought he was joking, but he was very serious. I said, "Sir, they're not going to hold the plane. They just don't do that."

Still, he didn't believe me. He asked that I call the airline and said that he'd be right down. Sure enough, as I got the representative on the phone, he approached the desk. I gave him the phone and he said, "I need you to hold the plane. This is Dr. Calloway and I'm scheduled to fly back home today but I'm running late."

He stood there for a few moments before he handed me back the phone with a puzzled look on his face. "You're right. They don't do that."

Where's the Porn Shop?

A gentleman approached the concierge desk and asked me where the porn shop was. Now, many concierges in Vegas might have replied, "Sir, there are several. Take your pick," but there was a large porn convention in town at this time, so I knew immediately that that's what he wanted to locate. I gave him the directions and he thanked me, and was off.

A few hours later, the same guest came back to the desk. "Excuse me, but why did you send me to a pornography convention? I asked you where the porn shop was." I stood there confused, thinking I'd been wrong. Perhaps he'd really wanted a particular shop. Then he clarified.

"You know, like the television show, Porn Stars?" After a second, I realized my mistake and immediately became embarrassed. The man's accent had turned 'pawn' into 'porn.' He'd wanted to visit the popular Pawn Stars shop that had been on television, and I'd given him directions to one of the largest pornography conventions in Vegas.

Do Not Try to Understand

Some concierge desk calls simply defy common sense.

A male guest in his early thirties said he was having trouble getting out of his room. "What's the problem sir?" I asked. He explained that the only door he could find had a sign hanging on the knob that read, 'Do Not Disturb.' "Where is the exit?" he asked innocently.

I'm not sure if it was the booze, the drugs or the gambling losses, but this guy literally thought that the 'Do Not Disturb' sign hanging on the inside of his door, designed for his use, was instructing him not exit his own room. Once we gave him permission to ignore the D-N-D command, he was happily sprung for, presumably, more partying.

As far as I was concerned, I could have used at that particular moment a sign of my own. One that said, simply, 'Do Not Understand.'

What Goes Up...

A lot of guests ask about the Eiffel Tower experience at the Paris Hotel and Casino. I like to reply that it is a pay-as-you-go, self-guided tour through a half-scale replica of the famous French landmark.

For one couple, this overview clearly was not sufficient. "So how do we get to the top?" the wife asked. "You take a glass elevator ride to the summit," I replied, adding that they should be sure to bring a camera to photograph the twinkly nighttime tapestry of Las Vegas.

We talked a little bit more about the experience, and the couple was preparing to walk away when the wife said, "Okay, so we take the elevator up but how do we get down?"

For a moment, I thought about suggesting his-and-hers parachute rentals. The woman had a bit of a giggle at herself when I smiled warmly and reassured her that the elevator goes down as well as up.

Barking Up the Wrong Acronym

I once had an older gentleman checking in who wanted some details about the entertainment in Vegas. "Will you be staying through Saturday?" I asked.

"What?" he asked. "Will you be staying through Saturday?" I repeated. "Oh, yes," he said.

"Wonderful. And did you have any specific plans in mind for your stay; maybe a show or dinner?" I asked. "What?" he replied. So, I repeated myself again. Just then, he leaned forward and said, "You should know that I have AIDS."

As you can imagine, I felt terrible. It took me a moment to gather myself. "Oh, sir. I'm so sorry to hear that."

After looking at me for a few beats, he said, "No, no. Not that kind of AIDS. Hearing aids." He pointed to each ear and turned his head in both directions to display the contraptions. For the rest of our conversation, I spoke loudly, all the while keeping a serious case of laughter under wraps. As soon as the man had checked into his room, I was able to have a good chuckle at myself, along with feeling relieved that my newly acquired guest wasn't sick!

Propositions

Unusual Requests

Most Las Vegas concierges won't blink an eye at some of the requests that ordinary people might find a little strange. It's all part of the job, whether it's going out to find a strange food in the middle of the night or finding tickets to a specific show. However, as you'll quickly see, some of the requests made of a concierge stick in their minds for a long, long time.

A Little Bit Allergic

I received an e-mail from a man who would be arriving at our hotel, and who would be staying for less than 24 hours. The e-mail started off normally, inquiring as to whether or not transportation was available from the airport. At that point, the man began describing issues that might affect his stay. I was informed that he had a 'very weak immune system,' and that he was at risk for collateral damage. His allergies included cigarette smoke, molds, fungus, yeast, wheat, oats, barley, rye. He couldn't be around any smokers, because they 'shed whatever he was allergic to.' He explained that he was 'anaphylactic' towards any type of shellfish.

In addition to all those allergies, he also couldn't have any type of dairy product, including anything that contained whey or caffeine. He was highly allergic to chocolate, artificial sweeteners, and in his own words, 'essentially allergic' to alcohol. He could not tolerate spices other than salt and pepper, and was worried about food transfers.

He was allergic to synthetics and required only cotton sheets. He could eat only broiled meats, fresh fruits, steamed vegetables, eggs, and water. After this massive list that spelled out everything the man couldn't tolerate, he let us know that his wife would appreciate it if he arrived home safely rather than in a pine box. He also asked if we had adequate facilities and whether he should come prepared for the worst case scenario.

I'm happy to report that we accommodated this man very nicely, and we were able to provide him with everything he needed... and that he went home by airplane, and not in a pine box!

Just Say Cheese

I had the chance once to meet a very famous boxer who was a super-nice guy. Off duty, I ran into him at a popular Vegas night club. I sat at his table, and everyone who passed stopped to say hello to him; he was very well-known. Throughout the night, he's drinking continuously and at one point, he approaches my friend and me and says, "Can you get me out of here?"

Always a concierge, my desire to serve kicked in even though it was my night off. Of course, I ask, "Where is your room?" He shakes his head and says, "I don't want to go to my room. I want to get a grilled-cheese sandwich." He names a very popular fast-food chain, and gets his money out of his pocket to tip us. I want to take this man to get his grilled-cheese sandwich, but I keep thinking of my car outside; a two-door, little Honda that had seen better days.

Reluctantly, my friend and I lead him to the car and put him in the backseat. I can't believe that I have a world-famous boxer who has just dropped several thousand dollars in a night club, ducking his head in the backseat of my old car. We get him to the fast-food joint, and order his grilled cheese for him. It's hilarious, because instead of ordering a grilled-cheese sandwich from room-service, this boxer wanted the grilled-cheese from a specific chain.

It's one of the things I think about when people say money can't buy happiness. For some, a few dollars will buy happiness in the form of toast and melted cheese!

I've Got Zilch Babe

A woman guest got in touch with me and let me know that she required the contact information for a very famous celebrity's plastic surgeon. This particular celebrity, with high cheekbones and a long sheet of dark hair, is very beautiful. I spent hours searching the Internet, skimming through our personal resources, calling the plastic surgeons I knew. I even pulled some strings in the entertainment industry.

No one appeared to know who the plastic surgeon was, or if they did, they were keeping it secret. Apparently, this celebrity either doesn't want to share her plastic surgeon, or when she has surgery done, it's far from The Strip!

Puppy Love

A colleague of mine had a guest in his hotel (across the country), who wanted to send his girlfriend a gift for her birthday. She was staying in a very large hotel several hours from me. The attorney had purchased two adorable puppies that were waiting in a location near my hotel. He wanted them delivered to his girlfriend's hotel, and my colleague thought I could help make it happen.

The attorney had thought that perhaps a courier could deliver the puppies, but I didn't know of a single courier service that would agree to deliver animals. It was very important to the guest that the girlfriend receive her gift on her birthday, and we really wanted to make it happen. With the address and love note faxed over to me, I began making calls and trying to find a way to pull this off smoothly.

There was an adorable boutique store across the street, and I had them fashion these beautiful bows for the puppies. Finally, I was able to hire a limo driver to deliver the puppies to the girlfriend's hotel. He kept me updated during his eight-hour drive, and I contacted the concierge at the girlfriend's hotel. When the puppies finally arrived, that concierge attached the beautiful bows to the puppies and delivered them to the girlfriend's hotel room with the love note.

Through the efforts of three concierges working with different hotels, the puppies arrived at 11pm on the girlfriend's birthday!

Pretty in Pink

One of my colleagues received a crazy request from a very eccentric female guest back in the 80's. Then again, which one of us didn't receive a crazy request in the 80's?

This particular guest had a very spoiled little dog that she was very fond of. The dog trotted alongside her around the hotel – and, for that matter, all over the city – outfitted in tiny, custom-made, pink leather booties.

One very hot Las Vegas day, the guest decided that she wanted to take a swim and naturally, she expected to once again have the dog at her side. She called down to the concierge desk to request an inflatable raft that could comfortably accommodate both her and her dog.

My colleague found a suitable raft, but unfortunately, the dog's owner had not completely thought through this outing. As soon as the dog got near the pool, it jumped in, immediately ruining those beautiful little pink boots. In short order, we were on the phone to a local cobbler, ordering another expensive custom-made pair. All in the name of fashion!

Flower Power

Sometimes we have to pull off some last-minute magic. Case in point: flowers. Occasionally, the ordered arrangements don't make it to the hotel on time, so we have to make do with what we can find at the local grocery store. We pick the boldest, freshest flowers, buy the most modern vase we can find, and then cut and arrange the flowers to fit. No one's ever been anything but thrilled.

But here's a dirty little secret. More than once, when there is nothing suitable at the local grocery, we have had to make do with some very creative solutions. For example, one week we had a wedding party staying at the hotel and when the boutonnieres they'd ordered arrived, the flowers for the gentlemen turned out to be all wrong.

We called every florist we knew, but with the wedding just hours away, our only option was to buckle down and make the boutonnieres ourselves. While a couple staffers went to get necessities like pins and floral tape, I cut some roses from the bushes at the front of the hotel. We made eight boutonnieres in an hour and they looked completely professional!

Love is a Many Splintered Thing

A guest who wasn't actually staying at the hotel at the time called and put in a request that I will never forget. He said, "There's a lady who will check in tomorrow, and I'd like to surprise her." He wanted to have a poem written on the mirror in calligraphy, and it was important that the poem could be easily washed away once it was read. In an effort to help surprise the lady – let's call her Ms. Jones – I called housekeeping and asked if it could be done. Unfortunately, it couldn't.

So, I called the man back – we'll call him Mr. Smith – and explained that it couldn't be done. I offered to go out and get an inexpensive mirror that could be placed in the room with the poem painted on it. After letting him know that we could have housekeeping remove or clean the mirror after it was read, he agreed. He also wanted to add something; he wanted an illustration of a couple dancing placed next to the poem on the mirror. In addition to this, he wanted a specific song playing in the background, and a single rose placed next to the mirror.

With less than 24 hours to pull this off, I went out and bought the CD with the song, La Comparsita. I then rented a CD player from the audio/video department so that I could place the song on 'repeat.' With all that taken care of, I needed the most important thing – an artist who could create the illustration and the poem. At the time, we'd just had a beautiful mural painted in the hotel by a great artist and so I went to track her down.

Unfortunately, I was told that she was finished with the mural and had been gone for a week already. Bummer. I was walking back to my office trying to figure out how to put this request together when, lo and behold, I ran into the artist. She was coming to pick up her last paycheck! I cornered her and told her about the request. "But it will have to dry for a whole day," she told me, after I'd explained. So, I convinced her to do it right then and there!

With everything placed perfectly and the song playing in the background, I filled my colleague in on the situation because I'd be off the next day, which was a Sunday. However, that morning, I received a call from the concierge on duty, telling me that Ms. Jones was already at the hotel, and she was with a man, and the man was not Mr. Smith. I began to panic at this point.

We can't tell Mr. Smith that Ms. Jones has arrived, because Mr. Smith might be the husband. Or, perhaps Ms. Jones is here with her husband and Mr. Smith is a lover. It was a very awkward situation. I told the concierge to have front desk check Ms. Jones into a different room and then call her in her room. The concierge did so, and said, "Ms. Jones, we have a surprise for you, but it's only for you. If you could get away for a moment, the concierge will escort you to the surprise."

When the concierge opened the room for Ms. Jones, she began to cry. She was very moved, and said that the surprise was very beautiful. She then moved to the surprise room. (Mr. Smith had already paid for the upgrade.) When he called later to ask how the surprise went, we told him that Ms. Jones was extremely surprised and touched. Housekeeping took care of the mirror the next day. I'm still not quite sure what the situation was, but since then, I don't put anything into any guest's room if not requested by them specifically!

Getting All Lovey-Dovey

As a highly recognized symbol of love, commitment and purity, we get a lot of requests for white doves.

One time, I had a guest who wanted to propose to his girlfriend at the top of the Paris Hotel and Casino's Eiffel Tower. When he popped the question, he wanted us to release seven white doves behind him.

However, when we called the Paris to make the arrangements, they informed us that the camera hold wasn't big enough to capture seven white doves. At first, the guest was a little disappointed, but then he decided that releasing them in front of a fountain on Las Vegas Boulevard would do just as well.

Fortunately, one of our staffers had the presence of mind to call the SPCA. This quickly put an end to the planned stunt, because they informed us that the hotel would be responsible for the welfare of the birds and that in all likelihood, due to summer Vegas temperatures, the seven doves would fly around and eventually succumb to heat exhaustion.

Since none of us felt capable of trapping seven doves set free on Las Vegas Boulevard, and since we were equally reluctant to watch them crash and burn and then to have to answer to the SPCA, the guest had to make his proposal without the doves. In retrospect, perhaps one of the magicians headlining on the Strip at that time could have solved our quandary.

A Spectacular Art Show

When it comes to renting a personality to enhance a Las Vegas event, people tend to think of things like an Elvis impersonator or exotic dancers. But the truth is, everyone is for hire on the Strip. Even, if you have enough money, some of the big acts that perform nightly at the major hotels.

We once had a client who brought in some very expensive sculptures made by an artist in Laguna Beach, California. This woman wanted to present the artwork to her friends in as spectacular a fashion as possible.

So, after the sculptures were trucked in by the artist and artfully arranged around a swimming pool, we hired three acrobats to perform in the water as part of the official unveiling. The acrobats came in their full Las Vegas show regalia, which made for quite a contrast. To top things off, we also had a Brazilian samba band and catered food from a top-level South American chef.

All in all, our soiree turned out to be a delightful combination of art, music, performance and good food. An unusual sight in other parts of the country, perhaps, but here in Vegas, just another typical day on the Strip!

Prehistoric

Not too long ago, I was approached by a guest who was the Vice President of Sales of a huge international company. His first words to me were, "I know it is Vegas, and anything can happen in Vegas." As you might imagine, by his words, I guessed that his request was going to be quite interesting. "We have a sales presentation tomorrow in the conference center. What I need from you is a yellow dinosaur costume."

Sure, I expected a strange request, but I was not prepared for this! This man was well over 6 feet tall, and needed a yellow dinosaur costume by the next day. I should mention that it was Saturday night already, so my hopes of finding one weren't high. Still, I said, "I'll check into it and see what I can find, and I'll give your room a call as soon as I find something."

I called all the local party stores and costume rental stores, and most of them were already closed. However, I finally found a costume store that was open, and they just happened to have a purple dinosaur costume that was for a tall person. Even better, the owner told me they could probably dye the costume and make it yellow!

From the time the guest requested the costume, it took only 20 minutes to locate it. I was ecstatic, considering I didn't believe it could be done. The guest was over the moon as well. After locating the costume, I couldn't help but sit back a moment and agree with the guest's earlier statement, "Anything can happen in Vegas!"

The Perils of Passover

Due to the nature of the annual Passover holiday, we must make special accommodations each year for our Jewish guests.

Among my annual Passover visitors were a pair of lifelong male friends from New York, co-presidents of some huge company. They're the most charming guys you could ever meet and although they arrived each year with their families in tow, their big thing was to try and out-do the other with some sort of elaborate practical joke.

This one time, Max comes over to me discreetly and says, "I need a camel." Curious, I reply: "A cigarette or a real camel?" Max immediately gets a little annoyed, because for him and his target, joking is serious business. "A camel. Like *Lawrence of Arabia*. I need a real camel. And please, keep it confidential."

Forgetting about Max's trickster nature and thinking this is one of the more obscure Jewish traditions I had somehow missed out on before, I called everywhere I could think of and finally found someone close to Las Vegas willing to rent a couple of camels. They were delivered that night and once they arrived, I went and quietly got Max.

There they were out front, a pair of real live camels with two fellows in Bedouin outfits. Max took one look at them and doubled over laughing. "Oh, this is perfect," he gushed. "Follow me!" So he and I took the two Bedouin guys with their animals and parked them outside the villa where Max's friend Sam was staying.

Believe it or not, Max camped out all night in order to be there when Sam opened his door in the morning, and needless to say, it was worth it. Sam just about jumped out of his skin when he saw a pair of camels and a couple Bedouins just beyond his door. Very quickly though, Sam caught on to the joke and the pair thought this was the most hilarious thing they'd ever done to each other.

But that wasn't the end of it for the Bedouin guys. They convinced Max and Sam to sit on the camels for a photo opp, and as soon as they started posing for pictures, one of the Bedouin guys clicked his tongue and made the camels stand straight up. Max and Sam were holding on for dear life, screaming for the Bedouins to stop as they were led around the golf course.

It was a very odd sight. As the Bedouins traipsed around one of the holes with the camels, players stopped to laugh at Sam and Max. The duo were so relieved to finally be off the camels, they just put their arms around each other and started heading back to their villas. "Not so fast," I said. "Who's going to clean up all this camel dung?"

They knew it had to be them, and sure enough, it was. The whole thing ended with these two company presidents shoveling piles – and I do mean piles – of camel turds, with players on the golf course laughing even harder than before. Since then, Sam and Max still come to our hotel every year with their families for Passover. But they definitely don't prank each other the way they used to.

Birthday Blowout

I received a call from a lady who was in her 50's. She was coming to Vegas with a close group of her friends to celebrate one of the girls' 50th birthday. This guest wanted her friend's birthday to be extra special, so she wanted a limo to pick them up at the airport. She requested that champagne and chocolate-covered strawberries be in the room when they arrived. After the usual requests for dinner reservations and show tickets, the woman threw something on me that I wasn't expecting.

"I'd like to have a Frank Sinatra or Dean Martin-style singer greet us at the airport and then sing as we get our luggage," she said. "Ooh, also, I want a blow-up doll in my friend's room as a joke – inflated and ready to go, if you know what I mean."

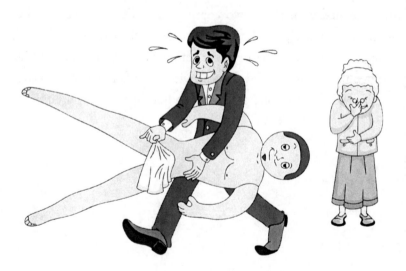

There I went, to the adult superstore, where I purchased the doll. Everything was going very smoothly up until that point. After I'd purchased the doll, I realized there was going to be no way I could blow the doll up by myself back at the hotel. The only option was to have the clerks at the store blow the doll up for me.

This meant that I had to carry the doll all the way back to the hotel and through the crowded lobby – fully inflated and 'ready for action,' so to speak! Perhaps the funniest thing of the whole situation was the fact that I got far less looks and glances than I expected. Maybe the sight of a concierge carrying a blow-up sex doll through a Vegas hotel was not as 'out of the ordinary' as I'd expected.

The Talented Bellman

While many times it's the concierge who pulls through for a guest at the last minute, at other times it's another hotel employee pulling through for the concierge. One of my colleagues and her sister were celebrating at our hotel. They were both wearing backless dresses, and my colleague wanted to have a picture of her sister painted on her back; like a tattoo. They looked around for a tattoo artist and couldn't find any. When they asked me, I did the same, to no avail.

Suddenly, I remembered that one of our bellmen was a particularly great artist. I found him quickly and asked if he'd be able to do it. In short order, he found some paint that would work on skin, and served up a gorgeous painted 'tattoo' of my colleague's sister. It was not only wonderful that we could find someone to do it, but it was truly amazing to watch him work!

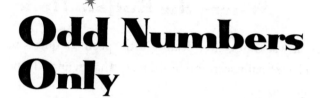

Odd Numbers Only

Very Unusual Requests

By the time a concierge has spent a year or two on the job, he or she might think that they've seen it all. They haven't! No matter how strange a request is, there's always one that will top it. The following stories will illustrate how even the most seasoned concierge can be blown away by guest requests.

Where the Buffalo Roam

It's easy at times, after dealing with specific requests to think that you have finally seen and heard it all. That is, until the next workday comes along.

A gentleman called down to my desk with what seemed at first like a straightforward request. "I need your help," he explained. "I am going to be attending an American Indian barbecue and I have been tasked with providing fuel for the fire."

I'm thinking, 'OK, mesquite charcoal, no big deal.' But this guy had other ideas. "I have to find a couple of bags of buffalo dumps. Do you have any idea where I can get something like that?"

Buffalo dumps, a.k.a. "meadow muffins" or "buffalo chips," are pieces of dried bison dung. Growing up on a farm in Texas where we used cow chips as Frisbees, I wasn't entirely foreign to this idea. I immediately called the caretaker of a ranch about two hours away. Although he laughed at my request, he told me if I made that two-hour drive to the ranch I could have all the buffalo chips that I wanted.

I forgot how strange it might seem for someone dressed as a professional concierge to be roaming the buffalo fields for droppings. Although I took off my formal, captain style jacket, there I was, in black vest and formal dress shoes, shoveling bison poop into garbage bags.

Once I had filled two huge trash bags and piled them into the trunk of the car, I thanked the caretaker and asked him if the hotel owed him anything for the buffalo souvenirs. "No way!" he replied with a big laugh. "I should be paying you for getting rid of the stuff."

I took the two trash bags back to the hotel and put them in the gentleman's room. After thanking me profusely for finding the buffalo chips (which no one thought I would ever find), he called my boss to sing the hotel's praises. "Your people are unbelievable!" he exclaimed. "Who the heck would have ever thought that somebody would go so far out of their way to shovel poop for me?" Who indeed?

Can You Hear Me Now?

A guest from South America came to the desk and asked if I could help him purchase two satellite phones. I thought, *Sure, we can do this.* I was imagining we could just run to the local communications store and pick a few up. Nope. That's not how it works. It turns out that satellite phones are only used by government officials, so it was going to be a serious challenge to get this man his phones.

I began wracking my brain to figure out who I knew that could help me assist this gentleman. I had friends who worked with a particular communications company, and they're the first people I called. Surprising me, they began asking questions about who this man was, and why he needed these satellite phones. I relayed exactly what the man had told me, "I understand that he's moving to a small island in the South Pacific, and because they don't have any telephones, he needs the satellite phones."

I have a feeling my friends suspected drug activity, but of course, I did not assume anything. Finally, I was given a number for a contact in the military who handled all kinds of equipment. I was able to set up a meeting between this contact and my guest. The phones were brought to the hotel, and the contact and the guest discussed them and looked them over a good bit. The guest ended up buying the phones (paying $25,000 each for them), and I was able to learn just exactly how one buys a satellite telephone. I'd be lying if I didn't say I felt pretty cool being able to locate these phones... another day in the life of a concierge, I suppose!

Getting Down and Dirty

Generally speaking, the major Las Vegas hotels like to bring in an outside company to handle the recycling aspects of their garbage. They pay, in some cases, thousands of dollars per month to have an external crew sort through the trash pile to parse out items like bottles, cans, and so on.

This kind of tidbit was part of an unusual tour we arranged for a member of a convention group. While his buddies were locked in on activities such as ATV races and skydiving in the desert, he for some reason asked for a tour of our hotel's trash cans and compacting capabilities.

He got a good look at the underbelly of the hotel beast and also asked a number of interesting questions – What was the most shocking item ever found in the trash? Has anyone ever fallen down the trash chute? And so on. Maybe next time, he can check out the laundry facilities.

In Loving Memory

The strangest request I ever received came from a guest who brought an urn full of his loved-ones ashes with him to the hotel. The gentleman was older, and had a very sweet demeanor. He explained to me that his loved-one had been very fond of Las Vegas. "I'd like to scatter his ashes on top of his favorite casino," and he named one of the most popular Vegas casinos.

I had assumed the negative outcome of every phone call I made, but I tried very hard to help this man fulfill his wish. Unfortunately, none of the casinos in the area would allow it. Imagine my reluctance to tell this man that it was impossible! He was disappointed, but apparently would not be defeated in this task. Purchasing a ticket for a popular roller coaster, the guest took the urn with him! By the time he stepped off the ride, the urn was empty.

80 Years Young

When you think of someone celebrating their 80th birthday, you might picture a small family celebration, discussing memories and enjoying cake, and perhaps singing a little bit. That was not the case with a particular guest of mine. Back in the 1990's, the Strip was still relatively low-key. An elderly guest who was staying with us had a desire to celebrate his 80th birthday in a peculiar way. He wanted to go skydiving.

At this time, there weren't a ton of thrill rides or places that I could actually approach. I finally tracked down a skydiving school in Boulder City who was a bit reluctant to take a man of my guest's age skydiving, but finally agreed. Many scenarios went through my head, and I wasn't even sure if the guest would actually go through with it! Turns out, he did and had a fabulous time.

In fact, he had such a great time that he wanted to go para-sailing! He even asked me to come along. I plainly (and jokingly) told him that I thought he was crazy, and I declined the invitation, but I made the arrangements for him. Again, he had a wonderful time.

The following year, he joined us again for his 81st birthday. I was quite nervous, sure I'd have to arrange for him to go bungee jumping or racecar driving. However, he decided to keep it simple with dinner and a show. I'm assuming he didn't want to 'show up' the younger family members that were staying with him!

Wardrobe Malfunction

We see a lot of unbelievable shows and conventions working at Las Vegas hotels. I remember one day a comedy troupe came through to perform at a convention party in one of the ballrooms. They were a special group, very much Avant-garde in their comic styling, employing a lot of magic and special effects in their act. They arrived and began to prepare for their show. Everything seemed to be in perfect order until they realized that one of their props had gone missing: a straitjacket!

Now, a straitjacket is not the most accessible prop, even in a town known for its many and varied shows like Vegas. They hadn't been used practically for almost two decades by then, as they were deemed medically inhumane, and we sure did not have one lying around. Still, it was an important part of their act, and it was up to me and my staff to procure one before curtain time. The prospect of locating a straitjacket so close to show time left us nonplussed, to say the least. We were freaking out!

Then I had a bit of an epiphany and said, "Let's call the larger hospitals in the area." I knew that hospitals had little areas near the IR, and special procedures to deal with those patients with drug and alcohol abuse problems that could not be controlled by conventional means. "Maybe some of them have straitjackets for extreme cases," I thought, "Something to hold the drunks in before they are taken to a rehab facility."

I knew someone over at one of the larger hospitals and called him. "We don't use them anymore," my friend informed me, "but I'll take a look." It took some time, but my friend took some people to look over some old, forgotten storage rails in some back room of the hospital, and eventually found one. And none too soon! I sent a runner over there, and we had the straitjacket on the prop table, twenty-five minutes before the curtain went up!

We were worried for a while there, but it all worked out, and we all learned one valuable lesson: nothing is too outrageous in this town, so always expect the unexpected. I may never need it, but I always make sure to keep a straitjacket around just in case.

For Russia with Love

I had this guest approach me one day and, before even introducing himself, he slapped down a crisp $100 bill on my desk. "Tennis, dinner, a show," he exclaimed. "I need you to set me up today with the works."

Every day thereafter, it was the same drill. He showed up at my desk, produced a $100 bill and told me what he needed. Finally, on the fifth and final day of his stay at the hotel, he showed up and announced that he had something a little more difficult in mind for the grand finale. 'Oh boy,' I thought to myself. 'Here it comes, a request for a contract killing.'

"Joe," he announced, "I need you to find me a contractor to build my hotel." This was perhaps the strangest request I had ever received as a concierge. "I own land in Sochi, Russia, the town where they will be holding the 2014 Winter Olympics. Your hotel here in Las Vegas is so beautiful, I would like to hire the same people to build my hotel. I have the plans and everything else done. I just need a contractor to get the ball rolling."

By the time my guest had left the next day, I had managed to set up a conference call with a Boston company for the following week in Hawaii, where he was headed next. In the end, the deal did not go through, but my guest was very thankful nonetheless. I was just happy to have helped him... and glad I ended up calling contractors rather than assassins.

Breast Milk

As a concierge, you become accustomed to guests requests, so much so that you begin thinking of how to accommodate them almost before they've finished asking the question. Once, I had a female guest call down and said, "Could you get me some breast milk, please?". Before it registered in my mind that there was no possible way I could bring this woman some breast milk (regardless of what she wanted it for, which is still a mystery to me), I thought, *Now who do I know that is lactating?*

Tiger in the Bathroom

Many guests make requests based on their favorite Las Vegas movies. For instance, a lady contacted me with an idea to mimic the movie, *The Hangover.* She wanted a real, live white tiger placed in the bathroom so that it would scare her husband when he opened the door! Of course, I had to tell the woman that it was impossible due to liability issues.

"What's the next best thing?" She asked me. So, I called over to a particular casino and I ordered a huge, stuffed white tiger. As the couple entered their room, the husband turned on the bathroom lights to receive quite a start! I couldn't help but wonder what went through his mind when she told him how she'd tried to get a real tiger placed in their bathroom to scare him... ah, the things we'll do for love!

Special Delivery

A Japanese couple came to me with a request one day. The man asked me a question, and I assumed I'd misheard him because he had a very thick foreign accent. When he repeated himself, I realized I had NOT misheard. "I need bull testicles."

"Ok-ay," I said, a big smile plastered on my face, hopefully hiding the wide-eyed panic starting to set in. They explained to me precisely what they needed and it turns out that testicles are a delicacy in Japan. They wanted to ship some to some friends back home. I called a few delis in town, and you can imagine the responses I received.

Suddenly it hit me that there was a rather large ranch in California, not too far away. I just assumed that they must have bulls, and where bulls are, there testicles be. So, I called them immediately and found out that they did in fact have the testicles we needed. The guests were thrilled, and I was then set to the task of arranging shipping. The couple paid about $8,000 for the testicles and $3,000 for shipping.

For days, my co-workers wanted to know just how big the testicles were, and whether I'd tried this delicacy or not. I quickly informed them that I had not sampled them, but that I could provide them with the contact information of the ranch if they were so curious about size and taste!

Stolen Wallet

A guest called down in quite a state to tell me that someone had stolen his wallet. I said, "I'm so sorry, Sir. Let me transfer you to security."

"No, no. Wait. Before you do that, I want you to know that I know who did it" the guest said. Thinking that this was great and that the police would have more success if the perpetrator's identity was known, I said, "Oh great. Do you want to file a police report?"

"No!" the man said quickly. Confused, I said, "Oh. Was it one of your friends?"

"No. It wasn't a friend," the guest replied. As I'm standing there trying to figure out who the man could be protecting by refusing to file a police report, he finally got to the point. "The truth is, I got a hooker last night and she stole my wallet! I don't know how to get in touch with her."

Dumbfounded, I was thinking, *Oh my! There's no way I can track down a prostitute to try and locate this poor guy's stolen wallet.*

Finally, I said, "I'm so sorry, Sir. There's no way I can help you, though. We're not permitted to address those kinds of issues. I'm sure you understand." Without so much as a thank you, the man hung up. To this day, I wonder what that man expected me to do!

Ante Up

Money Matters

Money can allow people to fulfill their strangest desires, and in a Las Vegas hotel, this usually requires the help of a concierge. This often puts those concierges into hilarious, uncomfortable, or fascinating situations. Most of all, guests with tons of money and odd requests make for memories that are not easily forgotten.

Catering to a Texas Cinderella

Smaller boutique hotels offer the chance for a more intimate rapport with guests. One of the guests I remember best was a Texan woman who was the poster child for 'bigger is better.' She had big hair, a big voice, and lots of big personality. Everyone was 'darling' to her, and every time she walked into a room, she sent heads spinning.

On one occasion when she was checking out, she asked me to take care of something for her before her plane left at 7pm that night. She'd seen a pair of gold Manolo Blahnik shoes during a previous visit to New York and now wanted me to locate a pair of these same shoes in Vegas.

I immediately got to work, searching the internet and calling boutiques and shops. Eventually, I got in touch with a local merchant who had one pair of the shoes I needed, and in the perfect size! The price tag was about $800. I told the store's concierge my story, and emphasized how badly my guest wanted these shoes. I had 45 minutes left to get those shoes, and I wasn't going to take no for an answer. The concierge was very sweet though, and told me he'd bring them over.

So, my Texan lady was eating dinner when the concierge arrived with her shoes. I was so excited to have gotten them that we walked right into the hotel restaurant; I took off her shoes and put the Blahniks on. She was so happy that she actually started crying like she'd just hit the lottery! She'd expected me to get a store name, perhaps a number for her, but here I was slipping her coveted shoes onto her feet. It really felt like a fairytale.

It was one of those perfect moments where I was able to not only deliver, but over-deliver. Smiling up into her ecstatic face, I happily told her that the shoes were absolutely 'darling.'

An Aussie Adventure

Arranging luxurious stays for wealthy guests and their entourage is a big part of any Las Vegas concierge's job. However, sometimes there's an entirely unexpected twist to these sorts of proceedings.

I once worked with an Australian gentleman who wanted nothing but top-of-the-line accommodations for himself and his four mates. He booked a brand new $40,000-a-night suite and asked for extras like a drum set, an electric guitar, a bass guitar and a humidor filled with Cuban cigars. (Since the last item was illegal, we enlisted a Cuban staff member to roll cigars for them.)

He also flew in a personal stylist from New York who, armed with the measurements of each soon-to-arrive guest, filled the suite's closets with the latest in top-name fashions. The head of the Aussie party paid for the stylist's first-class round trip airfare, hotel room, meals at five-star restaurants and outrageous fee for her work.

For three days straight, these five Australians went on helicopter tours, sat VIP at shows on the Strip and did meet-and-greets with the casts. They also celebrated one of the guy's birthdays at a local spa at sunset, with cake and only the best champagne.

I thought nothing of it until several months later, when I read in a magazine that the very same Australian magnate had been arrested Down Under for embezzling millions of dollars. Turns out he was playing with house money.

Man Overboard

"I want the very best, and money is no object." How many times have we heard this? Whether it's the queen's treatment at the spa or the most elaborate wedding proposal ever, many guests will tell a concierge to think nothing of the cost. On some occasions, it becomes clear that the guest hasn't thought too much about the cost either!

Such was the case when a young guest strolled over to me many years ago, girlfriend in tow. "Hey," he said. "I'd like to go on a cruise... a private cruise for a week. On a yacht."

I could already hear the 'cha-chings' of charges sounding in my head. "That will be quite expensive," I replied, hesitantly. "I don't care," he said. "I'll pay whatever it costs." I nodded, and he asked me to call his room when I'd collected the information. After making the calls he requested, I rang his room. "The cost of the private cruise will total about $3,000 per day," I told him.

"What?" He was incredulous. "I'd expected to pay that much for a whole week on board," he said. I told him I was sorry and that he must have been thinking of a commercial cruise line. "Would you like me to book the private yacht for you sir?" I asked. The man declined exuberantly.

I quickly learned that sometimes, "whatever it costs" is a bigger bite than some guests are prepared to chew!

Bowled Over by a Biker Dude

With one guest who told me there was no monetary limit, I suspected things would be different once he discovered the price of what he wanted. Everything about this guest screamed 'eccentric.' He wore a Harley Davidson t-shirt with shorts, and socks that were pulled up to his knees. His beard was shaved in odd, angular edges. He was quite a character!

"Today is my girlfriend's birthday," he said to me. "I intend to take her to the nicest restaurant you can think of. Money is no object. I don't care what it costs." I was already getting that dreaded feeling in my stomach, because the nicest restaurant I could think of was very pricey, indeed. However, as a concierge it's my duty to do as requested. "Absolutely," I replied.

I made reservations at a nearby restaurant which was the absolute top of the line; beautiful atmosphere, delicious food, rustic yet elegant setting. The whole time I was feeling bad about the possibility of canceling later. A few minutes later, I received a phone call from a salesman with a local luxury car dealership. "I'm calling to confirm a delivery," he said. "One Ferrari and an Aston Martin for a Mr. D-."

I'm not ashamed to say that my jaw dropped open. As I was picking it up off the floor, I took a second to Google my eccentric guest's name, and there he was – a famous collector who regularly spends millions of dollars on luxury vehicles. He'd obtained more than a hundred of them.

When the cars were delivered, Mr. D- chose the Aston Martin, and drove his girlfriend to dinner at that gorgeous restaurant. I'm still trying to decide who was more impressed, me or the girlfriend!

A Harem of Suitcases

We had a very wealthy Saudi guest arrive in Las Vegas on his private jet. I am not exaggerating when I say he did not pack lightly. He had a wonderful stay, and apparently enjoyed shopping quite a bit. When he was prepared to leave, we were in for quite a surprise. With the luggage he'd brought with him and the things he'd ended up purchasing during his stay, this man had 98 suitcases to take home!

We had nowhere near the necessary amount of bellboy staff or trolley equipment to handle this man's 'baggage,' so we had to rent a large, specially made luggage tube to transport his suitcases from the hotel back to his airport. This still stands as the record, at least from my personal point-of-view, as the highest number of bags attached to a single Las Vegas visitor.

In fact, in all my years as a concierge, I've never seen a shopping-addicted wife, a touring musician, or a fashion-conscious athlete come even close to beating our Middle Eastern VIP.

Leaving on a Jet Plane

Eccentric guests are always a challenge and if they happen to be a billionaire, it just adds to the challenge or it is another level all together. One of the things I found myself doing for this guest was traipsing to an infamous department store every single day to purchase brand new underwear. Why? Because this man never wore the same underwear twice! I thought this was going to be the strangest or most surprising thing about him, but I was wrong.

The man was interested in a particular piece of land for cattle, and he needed a flight from the hotel to that area. The problem with the commuter planes that routinely went to the target area was that there were no bathrooms on board. So, my guest approached me and he said, "I need you to find me a plane."

"What type of plane?" I asked. "I don't care," he replied, and then he leaned in a little closer, adding, "as long as there's a bathroom on it. I need it to be a jet."

"Okay, I'll look into chartering a jet," I told him. "No, no. I'm going to buy the plane," the guest replied. I was quite taken aback, but I told the guest I'd look into it. I began calling around the private airport and asking questions. I said that I didn't know how serious the guest was, but that I needed to know whether there were any jets for sale. Surely he's pulling my leg, I thought.

About 2 hours later, I was finally in touch with an agent for the private airport, who came to the hotel. He met with my guest, who then purchased the jet for several million dollars! Obviously, he had not been kidding. As he left to check out the land he was interested in, I couldn't help but hope that after all that, he formed a better attachment to the jet than he did his undies.

Oil Magnate

There are many fascinating things you get to behold in this business, and absolutely insanely-rich guests are included. I'll never forget the time a Texas oil billionaire stayed with us. His main bodyguard carried around a leather bag stuffed full of $100 bills.

I accompanied him to a Las Vegas nightclub for a birthday party. The man was in no way reserved with his money, and tipped the security guards, the servers, the hosts – everyone. When I say tipped, I mean, several hundred-dollar bills at a time. He bought $5,000 bottles of champagne like they were dollar souvenirs. My eyes nearly fell out of my head at how much money this man was handing out.

He'd booked the most expensive suites in the hotel, complete with private infinity pools, massage rooms, etc. As I was escorting him back to these suites at the end of the night, my head was absolutely spinning. Doing quick math, I knew that the man's nightclub excursion had cost at the very least $125,000. I just kept thinking that it would take me almost three years of working and saving every single dollar to make the amount of money that my guest had handed out in the course of a few hours!

Putting on a Side Show

One thing I've learned as a concierge is that if you have enough money, amusing yourself is not a problem. I once had a very rich businessman from Europe staying in my hotel, in a two-story penthouse suite. We'd handled all kinds of things for this man, but on one particular evening, he says to us, "I have a surprise in my room that I'd like to show you. When you have a moment, please come on up."

He was chuckling a bit, and of course, this left me wondering what in the world the surprise was. When I was on break, a couple of colleagues and I headed up to the guest's suite. On the bed were two little people, knocking the tar out of each other with pillows. The room was filled with the guest's friends, who were watching the fight with amusement, and possibly even betting on the outcome.

Several things were flashing through my head – like how in the world this guest had managed to find little people who were willing to pillow fight, and what had made him even think to do it – but mostly, I was just thinking, Oh my god! There are little people pillow fighting in here.

After a few moments, I politely thanked the guest for showing me the night's entertainment, and then excused myself from the room. I have no idea how much he'd paid the little people to pillow fight, but I have a feeling they made out like tiny bandits.

Gambling on Love

Love and Marriage

One of the most touching things about being a concierge is getting to be a part of intimate life moments between guests. Whether it's helping to set up the perfect proposal or assisting in the creation of a divorce 'celebration,' you're able to witness moments that will forever change the lives of the guests involved. It can be very emotional, and most of these moments are ones that concierges keep close to their hearts.

Gondola Ride

I had a guest who was planning the perfect proposal. We'd helped him with everything – from roses and the limo to a show and dinner reservation. The groom wasn't finished though. He really wanted to take his girl for a Gondola ride to the Venetian Hotel, but there was no way to make a reservation – it was first come, first serve. The guest had a super-tight schedule, and he didn't think he was going to be able to get away from his girlfriend long enough to arrange it. Of course, he was nervous and anxious.

So, I said, "I'll go and pay for the ride, and you can just reimburse me." I was so caught up in the proposal that I couldn't stand the thought of him missing his chance to get the Gondola ride. He wasn't sure how long it would take him, and I ended up booking two consecutive rides, just in case the waiter was late with the bill or something else came up.

Luckily, the couple made it in time, and he asked her to marry him. She was overwhelmed and very touched, and of course she said yes. What I thought was really sweet was how the guest told his fiancée how I'd helped him plan the entire thing. He could have easily taken credit for it all, but chose to recognize my help. I was touched as well, and couldn't help thinking that if he kept that kind of thing up, the two of them would be married for a long time!

Till the Garbage Disposal Do Us Part

Most people know how joyous and exciting a marriage party or reception can be. It's a wonderful occasion, but at a hotel in Las Vegas, I learned that there's something to be said for divorce parties as well. I was made aware that one of our permanent residents wanted help with a party to celebrate her divorce. This was certainly something new to me, but without judgment, I began making arrangements. At first, the idea was novel and cute, a sort of way to stay positive about things.

Instead of beautiful fresh blossoms, we began with a bouquet of dying, withering flowers, symbolic of the life that she'd had with her ex-husband. These were placed in 'his' area, on the table where he had handled the bills. Also in that area were the blackest, dreariest decorations available while her side of the room was celebratory and Barbie-pink.

There was certainly some humor interjected as the woman and her friends gathered samples of the food the ex-husband liked (dishes or meals she wouldn't have to cook anymore if she didn't want to) and dumped them down the garbage disposal. A fake ring was tossed down there as well, symbolizing the union which was now dissolved. The friends took the real ring and created a beautiful new pendant for the woman (a symbol of the transformation that the woman had undergone).

Along with that, one area of the room was lined with things that the ex-husband liked and objects that reminded her of him. She walked past these items; past the dirty clothes she would no longer have to wash, the things she would no longer have to endure. She emerged through a bunch of colorful balloons that were symbolic of her newfound freedom and the things she would devote it to; going on a cruise, learning to paint, playing golf.

It was probably then that I realized the woman emerging from the balloons really was a new woman completely; one committed to looking forward and making the best of her life. What had started as a cute and even tongue-in-cheek celebration actually made a lot of sense to me. It was a fantastic way to acknowledge that even with something like divorce, that is traditionally considered 'bad,' there is certainly a silver lining.

Just Remarried

With easy access in Las Vegas to drive-through wedding chapels, it's *the* spot for couples who want fast and beautiful weddings. For a couple of guests of mine, it was a perfect chance to renew their vows after years and years of marriage. Because the couple's family was scattered around the US, they decided to have fun with the renewal and go to one of the drive-through chapels. So, we made the arrangements and ordered a small cake for the couple to celebrate with after the renewal.

After the ceremony was already scheduled, I received a call from one of the kids of the couple. This man knew that his parents were planning to renew their vows, and wanted to plan a sneaky little surprise of his own. So, I went behind myself and re-configured the celebration to accommodate the man's own ideas for his parents' renewal.

At the appointed time, the couple pulled up to the drive-through wedding chapel. As they prepared to renew their vows, they saw swarms of bicycles come around the corner of the chapel and line up behind them. It was the couple's children and grandchildren, having all shown up to support the couple. Everyone was emotional and crying, and it was a wonderful surprise!

Later, the children and grandchildren fashioned signs that read 'Just Re-Married' and attached them to a pair of the bicycles. The 'bride and groom' rode up and down the Strip sidewalks, getting best wishes from strangers. I love that this couple had fun with their renewal, but that their family was able to make it so much more touching. I especially love that I was able to help out with such a wonderful memory!

Painting the Room Red

"I need your help," a guest called down and said to me one day. "I need to order 24-dozen roses for my room," he said. I chuckled and said, "You mean you want to order 24 roses, or 2-dozen?"

"No," he replied. "I mean 24-dozen."

When I didn't answer right away, he said, "Do you think that will be overwhelming in my room?" That's when I realized that he sounded a bit nervous. I said, "24-dozen roses are going to make your room look like a botanical garden!" He was in one of the smallest rooms in the hotel.

"That's what I want," he said. "I want to propose to my girlfriend, so I want her to be overwhelmed." Well, if that didn't just tug at the heartstrings! So, I said, "I'll make some calls." He was planning on taking his girlfriend out that afternoon and coming back by 5pm, so I had about 7 hours to get this done.

I made a call to the florist, who attempted to correct me in the same way I'd tried to correct the man. "Nope," I said. "He really wants the 24-dozen roses." It ended up costing the guest $3,000 for the roses (still the biggest order that florist has received to date), and we ordered both long-stem and short-stem roses.

When the man and his girlfriend returned, they walked into a room that was absolutely painted red by roses. They were arranged on the tables, placed in the bathroom, draped across the dresser – they were everywhere! He called down later to thank me, saying that the room had looked amazing and that his girlfriend had said yes. I thought, *well, with that display, I'd have said yes too!*

In the Navy

I'd seen a lot of men and women in uniform come to Las Vegas before or after posting abroad – to make the last few days count or to celebrate a safe, happy return.

A young Navy recruit came to me one day, explaining that he wanted to propose to his small-town sweetheart before he shipped out to Iraq. Never having traveled to a large city before, the man had no idea about how to propose in a large resort town like Las Vegas. He hadn't even purchased the ring!

He was incredibly sweet, always saying, "Yes Sir," or "No Sir. I helped him figure out exactly how he wanted to propose, and even pointed him in the direction of an affordable jeweler. When the big night arrived, he approached the concierge desk and asked me to fix his tie. He was wearing his blue navy dress uniform, and was so charmingly nervous! I felt like I was watching a romantic movie.

His girlfriend came down, and she was wearing a beautiful evening gown, but of course, was clueless about the proposal. I knew from helping the guy plan everything out that he was going to propose at the restaurant, where I'd arranged for the ring to come out with dessert. Then they would retire to their suite to celebrate with a bottle of champagne and roses. Later, they'd see a romantic show.

When the guest came back from dinner, he was in tears. At first, I thought the worst, and was nearly heartbroken. I asked him if he was okay. But, it turned out that they were tears of joy, because his girlfriend had said yes. He was choked up, and he was trying to thank me for my help. Here he was, so young and innocent and polite, about to go off to defend our country... I was very moved.

I finally convinced him that helping him had been an honor, and to accept it as my own small way of supporting his bravery – both as a soldier and as a man in love!

Australian Wedding

We often deal with marriage proposals. The usual is a romantic dinner and a nice show, but one guest had a request that was very out of the ordinary, and it didn't quite turn out like the storybook marriage proposal. I'd been working as a concierge for 12 years when this guest approached me. He told me he'd been living with his girlfriend for 16 years and he was ready to get married. He was really nervous about asking, and he wanted to have the entire proposal and wedding in Vegas.

He explained that they'd be coming from Australia, and that he wanted me to plan the entire wedding. Now, this was all going to be a surprise to the man's girlfriend, so he wanted me to plan her whole wedding with no input from her at all. I thought, *you have GOT to be kidding me!* I may not know that much, but I know a woman's wedding day is one of the most important days of her life!

"You want me to arrange the entire wedding, minister and all?" I asked. "Yes," he said. "We're going to get married in the room. It can be something beautiful and simple – nothing fancy." Incredulous, I said, "What about the dress?" He replied, "You're going to choose the dress. I'll give you the size and some ideas of dresses she would like." I was absolutely blown away that this man was really asking this. But, I did as he asked, and I planned the entire wedding.

The process took about 4 weeks, with calls and e-mails back and forth between myself and the guest. After choosing the flowers, the minister, and other little details, I narrowed the dresses down to 3 and I sent him a picture. He replied, "Well, I really don't know that much about dresses, which is why I wanted you to choose." I was hoping to at least have him pick one of the three. No go; he left it up to me.

We chose a jazz musician because his girlfriend liked jazz, and got everything else prepared. It was very close by then and I was feeling very nervous. When the couple checked into the hotel, the woman got very sick with the flu. Since the couple was scheduled to be at the hotel for a week, I was able to push things back, and I sent the in-house doctor to her. I said, "Please, Doc... do whatever it takes to make this woman better!" He gave her antibiotics and vitamin shots. After 2 days she began to feel better so I made the reservation for the guest so that he could propose.

When he asked, she burst into tears. "I came all the way here from Australia, I've been sick," she said. "I've been living with you for 16 years, and just now you're asking to get married? You knew I wanted to do this at home, with my family around me. What were you thinking?" He just told her that he'd wanted to surprise her, but she said, "No way. Absolutely not."

As you can imagine, the guest was terribly upset and I felt absolutely awful. The next day, the girlfriend came down to the lobby and she said, "I heard that you bought me a dress. You are a man and you actually picked out one for me." I said, "Yes, ma'am. I did." I was really nervous now; sweating bullets. She asked if she could see it and I said, "Absolutely," and I took her to the storage area where the dress was. She stared at the dress for a long time and then she said, "This is unbelievable. This is exactly the dress I would have chosen." After a few more seconds she said, "You know what? I'm going to do it. I'm going to get married in Las Vegas."

And just like that, the wedding was on again. It was just the couple, the minister, and me as the witness. The whole thing was an absolute emotional roller-coaster – up and then down and then up again. The couple still returns sometimes to celebrate an anniversary, and they always find me. I was so happy that everything worked out, and as you can imagine, I began feeling very secure about my dress-choosing capabilities!

Fulfilling a Simple Fantasy

A guest of mine who wanted to propose to his girlfriend created an elaborate plan and wanted me to get 24-dozen roses for him by the next day. Each dozen needed to be a different color. He also wanted a violinist and an accordionist to play music when he and his girlfriend arrived in the suite. While the roses might be okay, the music had me panicked. I had to find both an accordionist and a violinist and make sure they could play together.

As I was calling around, putting together these arrangements, the guest hit me with another request. He wanted a cocktail waitress uniform for his girlfriend – just like the ones from the waitresses in the hotel! For this one, I had to go through hoops and get approval from the vice president of the hotel himself. The guest ended up having to purchase a uniform from the hotel.

Finally, I'd put together everything so that it would be perfect for the guest and his girlfriend. When the big night came, he carried her in his arms through the door to the suite. She was unbelievable surprised at all the flowers and the band. Then he told the little band to play louder, took the cocktail waitress outfit and his bride, and disappeared into the other room! Nobody saw them again that night, but the band played for three hours before taking their leave. They must have had a great time!

Every Picture Tells a Story

Anniversaries are another occasion we really enjoy handling at the concierge desk. I once got a call from a male guest who was bringing his wife to celebrate their 30th wedding anniversary. He wanted to do something very special for her; something that would illustrate how much he loved her. I thought for a while, and then I came up with an idea I thought would touch them both.

I got in contact with the guest and I asked him to send me pictures from throughout the 30 years with his wife. He complied, and I set to work with my plan. The couple had booked a 2,000 square foot room for their stay, which worked perfectly with what I had in mind. When the couple arrived and entered their room, they were immediately greeted with pictures of themselves when they first met. I had printed out the photos and placed them all in beautiful matching frames.

As they walked through the room, the pictures told the story of their relationship; their marriage, a cross-country move, holidays, and other special times. All of these memories just lined the walls of their suite. Though the husband had been hoping to surprise his wife, they were both touched at what I'd done. They came down to personally thank me for the surprise, and even asked to take a picture of me in their suite, surrounded by the pictures. I kept a copy of this one, to remember my own little part in their romantic story.

Back to Their Future

Las Vegas is known for unplanned weddings, but one such wedding really sticks out in my mind. A couple approached us at the desk one day and told us that they'd like to get married... that same afternoon, when they returned from lunch! It was a spur-of-the-moment decision, but they wanted to have their wedding right there in our lobby. Needless to say, we were a little in shock. We had a few hours to prepare an entire wedding. That wasn't the most shocking part of this story, though.

This couple had been high school sweethearts that had drifted apart. They'd both married other people, and although they had loved their spouses, they'd never stopped loving each other. It just so happened that both of them had become widows recently, and had unexpectedly ran into each other in Las Vegas.

Wanting to catch up, they'd agreed to get together and talk, but soon discovered that they were still very deeply in love. As they told us their story, I found myself engrossed, as if I were watching a romantic movie!

After hearing about how the couple had never stopped loving each other, every available person went to work preparing the wedding. We got the marriage license arranged, filled the lobby with fresh white flowers, and recruited one of the bartenders to play the piano. It was such a touching moment, how this couple had found each other again after all this time. We were all witnesses to the wedding – and to how true love never really dies! The couple still joins us every year for their anniversary.

Bludgeoned by Bliss

Celebrities aren't the only ones who get married in Vegas and then suddenly decide it was a bad idea. It's a town where it's super-easy to get drunk, easy to get married, and then fairly easy to get divorced. In Las Vegas, it's not so much live-and-learn as it is live-and-forget.

For instance, one night a male guest approached me, and he was visibly upset. It had been just one day since he and his girlfriend had tied the knot at a nearby chapel. Unfortunately, in that small space of time, she'd done something so unspeakable that he no longer had faith in the vows she took.

Of course, the guest was crushed. I tried to console him as I scheduled transportation for the following morning to the city courthouse. There, he would file an annulment. I also booked him a solitary ticket back home. This wasn't the first or last time that I transformed from concierge to marriage counselor, legal adviser and travel agent. As they say, you live and learn.

Gambling on Love

A lot of people want to propose to their partner in Vegas with a gambling theme. It's cute, but sometimes it can be tricky. One guest wanted to propose to his girlfriend at a card table.

I knew this was going to be tricky, because everything is strictly regulated by the gaming commission. We couldn't create a rehearsed or fake game because every game that takes place on the gambling floor has to be a live game. So we came up with the idea of having myself and a co-worker playing at the blackjack table where the couple was going to be, and arranged with the dealer and pit boss for the lucky lady to be presented with an engagement ring on her third winning hand.

When the couple arrived at the table, the boyfriend knew all about our ruse but the girlfriend was in the dark. We started to make small talk, asking things like, "Where are you from?" Then, on the woman's third winning hand, the dealer put a small box on the top of her chips and slid the pile across.

The woman asked, "What's with the box?" The dealer – and the boyfriend – played dumb, but when she opened up the box, she was thrilled. As she looked at the ring, her boyfriend got down on one knee next to the table and officially proposed.

By that time, people at the other tables had noticed what was going on. Everyone burst into applause as the woman said yes and one of our cocktail waitresses appeared with a chilled bottle of champagne. It was a simple set-up, but still very memorable. We made a toast and to my knowledge, the boyfriend kept our part in the whole operation a secret.

Gypsy Fortune Teller

Guests often want their proposal to be a great surprise and this gentleman was no different. He had the idea of getting a boat ready so that he and his girlfriend could go for a short cruise. On the boat is where he would propose to his girlfriend. To make it cuter, he wanted to 'accidentally' run into a gypsy fortune teller with his girlfriend on the pier. We hired someone who would act as the fortune teller, and made sure everything was right.

The boat was waiting, and the man and his girlfriend walked down the pier. There, they ran into the gypsy fortune teller. The man convinced his girlfriend to have her fortune read. When she did, the gypsy revealed that the young woman would take a short trip. "Also," the Gypsy said with twinkling eyes, "you should expect to be given a very serious proposal very soon."

Of course, the girl didn't think too much about it as she and her boyfriend prepared for their cruise. On the boat, though, when the man got down on one knee and proposed, the truth struck the woman and she realized what was going on. She was shocked, and in reward for clever thinking and planning, the man received a 'yes!'

Cadillac Limo

Renewing one's wedding vows is all too common, so it's only natural for guests to look for some local talent to assist with their plans. I received such a request one particular afternoon and set out on the traditional path. I found an adorable church outside the city, at the top of a hill. I ordered beautiful flowers and found a priest. The couple also wanted a limousine to drive them to the church.

A few days before the wedding, the couple was talking to me; telling me how long they'd been together and different things about their lives. The husband had a huge passion for antique cars, and had accumulated several. During his story, something clicked in my mind. I had met a local man who drove a beautiful, gleaming old Cadillac that he often used to take people to proms or other special events.

I called him up, and asked if he'd drive my guests to their wedding. On the day of their wedding, the couple watched the beautiful Cadillac drive up, and the driver (dressed in a tuxedo) got out and came around to open the door for them. They were so impressed and touched at this little detail I'd surprised them with.

The most wonderful thing about it all was that the Cadillac was 25 years old, and the couple was celebrating their 25th wedding anniversary. It worked out perfectly!

The Scandinavian Bride

There I was, in the middle of one of our hotel rooms, tending to a bride-to-be. Not an unusual situation, except in this case, the bride-to-be was completely naked.

She had come to me, a female concierge, for friendly fashion advice about her wedding day outfit, right down to her sexy, frilly lingerie. Although this tattooed, punk rock looking woman from Scandinavia stood naked in front of me without any concern or embarrassment, it still felt strange and awkward.

The awkwardness intensified for me when she finally donned the wedding gown and it turned out to be too small. The back was a tangle of ribbons, with the corseting effect completely lost. But instead of breaking down in tears, the guest calmly took stock of the situation.

"I had a feeling it was not going to fit," she said. "That's just the way things go sometimes. But that's OK..." The guest then proceeded to make magical use of her misfortune. She added a strategic rip here and a careful off-the-shoulder maneuver there, and in a matter of moments she had transformed herself into a pink-haired dazzler with edgy wedding dress to match.

Honestly, watching this Scandinavian woman go from naked to nuptial in a totally unique kind of way was one of the most powerful representations of love and commitment that I have ever witnessed. And I can't say that I was that surprised when the groom showed up wearing a one-of-a-kind neon green tuxedo. Rock on!

Stacking the Chips

It's Their Party

Some guests rely on concierges to plan fun parties, or come up with entertainment ideas, while others have created their own idea of fun and simply rely on the concierge to follow instructions. It's the latter of the two that can often send a concierge out on a wild goose chase, and make for some pretty funny and memorable times. As you'll see in the following stories, everyone has their own idea about what's fun and exciting.

Poking Fun at the CEO

A technology company in London planned to stay with us to celebrate what had been a very good year. They were bringing their key employees to Vegas to stay at our hotel and casino as an incentive for doing a great job. While you might picture a bunch of men standing around checking their computers and adjusting their ties, the reality is that these guys were as boisterous and playful as puppies – and they were out to have a great time.

The son of the company's CEO called in advance and let us in on a little plan of his to prank his father, all in good fun, of course. The son gave us a general idea of what he was planning, which involved swimming and a cabana. When the big day arrived, they brought the CEO out – in his tiny Speedo bathing suit – and blind-folded him. They had hired a little person and he was dressed in the same Speedo bathing suit, and they handcuffed him to the CEO.

Now, this was a Sunday and the area was absolutely packed with people, who were all looking on. As you can imagine, the difference in size – along with the alcohol, because everyone was drinking – made it a bit difficult to swim without the CEO and his companion looking completely silly. The whole entire group joined in and everyone had a great time.

The Amazing Scavenger Hunt

After just a few months at the concierge desk, I got a call from a Canadian groom-to-be who was a big fan of the CBS-TV reality show The Amazing Race. He and 79 of his closest friends wanted to take part in a Las Vegas scavenger hunt like the ones featured on their favorite program.

Although the future bride was a paraplegic confined to a wheelchair, he told me that she planned on running the full scavenger race course with the rest of them. As you might imagine, it took several months to prepare for this unusual event, especially since my Canadian friends were on a strict budget and had charitably raised the money for their trip.

I purchased large quantities of items to accommodate ten teams of eight people each, things like cameras, backpacks and water bottles. I thought my Amazing Las Vegas Race would also be of interest to the local newspapers as a topic of coverage, but surprisingly, I didn't get very far on that front.

We used a special software package to map out the itinerary of the scavenger hunt until we got thrown into a scavenger hunt of our own. The computer program crashed, we lost a big part of the customized information we had compiled thus far and had to go through tech support... in India.

Finally, on a hot, steamy August 31st, it was time for the scavenger hunt. The group's tight budget created a variety of sideline issues such as having to use donated concierge certificates and tickets to cover the cost of breakfast. The group – of which more than half were senior citizens – had to observe the rule of no cell phone,

Blackberry or other wireless device use. Also, for liability reasons, everyone agreed to limit themselves to taking public transportation.

Before we even got out of the hotel, the great uncle of the bride, a team leader, got separated from his group! We had to get security involved to find him and restart the scavenger hunt all over again. I was personally wondering if the team was considering canning him as the leader, but the show went on. At each stop on the Strip – the MGM Grand, New York, New York, and so on – the teams were given clues, questions and crazy tasks like dancing on Las Vegas Boulevard with a total stranger. So, we had these senior citizens approaching locals and tourists and asking them for a dance on the boulevard or a peck on the cheek!

At one point, two of the teams colluded and stole another group's notebook, which was absolutely hilarious, but forced us to intercede. These older people simply weren't playing around when it came to winning, even if it meant they had to cheat a little! But in the end, everyone had a wonderful time, culminating with a buffet at Main Street Station downtown. Best of all, I was able – after the scavenger hunt, the wedding rehearsal and the wedding itself – to donate the tip I received from the group to a fund set up to pay for the bride's stem cell treatment in China. She was paralyzed from the waist down because of a high school swimming accident.

She and her husband, as well as some of the others Canadians in this group, became great friends of mine, sending me things like ice wine and maple syrup. At the time, I was a brand new concierge and when I look back on this whole episode, I realize how many things could have gone wrong. Amazing!

Serenaded at a Strip Mall

A very sweet guest wanted to do something special for her husband. She wanted to serenade him in a very public part of the Strip – but she wanted to be able to sit down at a piano and play while she sang to him. The idea was sweet and romantic, but finding a place where the woman could play the piano in public proved to be rather difficult. To top it off, she wanted to do it around 2 in the afternoon, which cut out the obvious solution of a piano bar, as none of them opened until early evening.

I finally located a nearby shopping mall, where a major retailer on the second level had a grand piano. Thankfully, he thought the idea was great as well and turned out to be just as excited about it as I was. He couldn't have been nicer!

So, when the day came, the husband was sent on an errand to a particular store in the shopping mall. As people were strolling by and hanging out in this mall, the husband walked toward the store – which is also just by the piano. That's when she began playing her song. The husband laughed first at the fact that he had been fooled, but as his wife sang to him, he had tears in his eyes and was very touched.

The man sat down next to his wife, and to everyone's delight, sang the last verse of the song with her. The people milling about had stopped completely to watch the husband and wife duet, and as the song ended, they applauded wildly. It was a beautiful moment and couldn't have gone off better. The moment was definitely worth the trouble of finding the piano!

When In Vegas

I will never forget the Playboy Golf Tournament. I'd only been working at this particular hotel for about 2 weeks, and the hotel was scheduled to host this tournament, as well as different activities for the participants. Along with 150 gentlemen who arrived for the tournament, there were the Playboy bunnies, the Playboy Girls of Golf, and various models.

After the group had arrived, our Director of Casino Services announced that we were going to have a toga party. This was at about 4pm, and all of the girls needed toga costumes. We sent out employees, but this happened not long after Halloween, and there weren't many toga costumes to be found. In fact, there was only one or two available. After a lot of brainstorming, we ended up getting the older sheets from housekeeping, with the idea of creating custom toga costumes.

Keep in mind that most of the people who were helping had no idea how to make costumes – and we were faced with the task of making these custom togas for more than a hundred guests! Trust me, we were in a bit of a panic.

Luckily, I had some experience in the costume industry, so I knew enough to create passable costumes, but there was no way I could outfit all of these girls by myself. So, I recruited help from some of the hotel managers and directors. We grabbed buttons, ropes, all the decorative items we could find and armed ourselves with hot glue, pins, needles and thread, and staples!

It was a Friday evening, and all of our regular guests were there in addition to our Playboy Bunnies and the golf crew. The guests walking through must have thought it was hilarious that there were all these older hotel managers and directors in 3-piece suits running around stapling up these half-naked Playboy Bunnies – or on their hands and knees sewing and pinning these costumes on! All in all, we created 120 toga costumes in just over an hour. The girls had a great time and it was one of the best events the casino has hosted.

A Cinematic Celebration

Not too long ago a client called down to the desk wanting a suggestion for a dinner party. They had very little time to plan, but they wanted it to be special.

Since the movie "Julia and Julie" had just been released, I suggested that they try a Julia Child themed dinner party; everyone could bring a sample of one of her recipes to share. The guest was elated!

That night the party guests arrived with their dishes and when the dinner was over they took a limousine to see the movie. In the words of Julia Child, "Dining with one's friends and beloved family is certainly one of life's primal and most innocent delights, one that is both soul-satisfying and eternal." I certainly think the dinner party guests were delighted and satisfied.

Their Kind of Town

One of my guests was going to be celebrating her 80th birthday during her stay. Her family wanted to surprise her with something really special, and they let me know that she was a huge fan of Frank Sinatra. Well, Vegas is THE place to find excellent celebrity impersonators, so my idea was easily obtained.

I made reservations for the guest and her family at one of the finest restaurants in Vegas, and during her meal, the woman got a singing telegram. The person delivering the telegram was the Frank Sinatra impersonator, and let me tell you, this impersonator was excellent. He looked like Sinatra, he sounded like Sinatra, and was an absolute crooner. The woman was shocked and extremely happy, and the family was thrilled with my idea. I told them with a shrug, "Hey, it's Vegas..."

Kings of the Wedding World

I was pretty accustomed to the occasional outlandish wedding request thinking it's all part of the job. They're fun, both for the people getting married, and for me. The request that stands out most in my mind came from a couple who wanted to do the whole 'Viva Las Vegas' thing, complete with an Elvis impersonator and themed chapel for the ceremony. I thought, *well, this will be pretty easy.*

It was going to be a fairly small ceremony; just 10 to 12 others were attending. I began making arrangements for that night when the couple sprang a little surprise on me. They wanted to rent Elvis costumes for every single person attending the wedding! Renting a few Elvis costumes would have been easy, but I wasn't sure if I could find that many in just a few hours.

Within minutes after being told, I was running all over Las Vegas, cleaning out Elvis costumes from every party shop and costume boutique I could find. While the women dressing up were a bit pickier about the type of costume they wore, everyone looked really great! The ceremony was hilarious and I still keep a photo of the 'Elvis wedding audience' on my desk.

Love Floats

A couple was staying in one of the penthouse suites, and the woman went out for a day of shopping. From personal experience, I know that people who come to Vegas for a special occasion like to celebrate big. While the woman was gone, the man came downstairs and told us he was planning on asking his girlfriend to marry him. He didn't want an elaborate dinner or tickets to a sold out show; he wanted balloons.

It turns out that his girlfriend loved balloons, and he couldn't think of a better way to 'set the mood' for the proposal than to get some balloons and put them in the suite. I was touched by the simple gesture, and as I was getting the details of the types of balloons he wanted, I realized it wasn't quite as simple a gesture as I'd imagined.

The man wanted 800 balloons! So, after the shock wore off, I got to work. By the time the woman had returned from shopping, we had helium-filled balloons covering every single inch of the couple's townhouse suite. The ceilings were high, and with all 800 balloons in the suite, it created a truly breathtaking effect. Of course, the man asked his girlfriend to marry him after she took in the beautiful sight, and she said yes. There might have been a ton of helium in the room, but I imagine she was walking on air!

Designer Birthday

Guests often celebrate their 21st birthdays in Vegas; the perfect place to use that legal ID in nightclubs and casinos. One of my guests was staying with us to celebrate this memorable birthday, and her family wanted to really make sure she had a great time. This guest adored everything Louis Vuitton – and had accumulated quite a collection of sunglasses, shoes, handbags and other accessories.

I conspired with her parents, and we had the hotel bakery design a special cake. It looked exactly like a Louis Vuitton bag, right down to the monogrammed insignia, buckles, and straps. At the stroke of midnight, when a bottle of champagne and the elaborate cake was delivered to her table in the nightclub, the brand new 21 year-old was absolutely beside herself.

It was a fabulous night, and the guest had a wonderful time. I think the most memorable thing to me was the price of the cake. At $2,000 it was costlier than the designer purse it was made to resemble!

A Trail of Clues

One of the sweetest things I've seen was a Valentine's Day celebration. I had a man come in who wanted to do something for his wife that was outside the box; something really special. He and I chatted about it for a while and came up with a stellar idea. His wife, who was completely clueless, was picked up by a limousine on Valentine's Day. Confused, she got in the limo and found a note on the seat. It explained that she was being taken to her favorite restaurant for a complimentary, private lunch.

When she arrived at the restaurant, she was told that her meal had been paid for by a secret admirer. After her leisurely lunch, she was taken back home, where she received another note telling her to pack an overnight bag. The limousine driver then delivered her directly to our hotel spa, where she got the royal treatment.

I sent a driver to pick her up and after her spa session I personally escorted her to the restaurant where she and her husband had first met. It was obvious that she was not only flattered, but was thrilled at all the mystery and surprise. It was a very beautiful Valentine's Day that ended with chocolate-covered strawberries, chilled champagne and fresh roses in their room. I loved the fact that after all their years of marriage, the husband still knew how to be romantic, but I couldn't help wondering how he'd top it the next year!

Riding with Elvis

A guest called me one day, and told me that he wanted to celebrate his mother's birthday. Family would be gathering from many different states, and they wanted to do something very special. The guest's mother would be turning 80, and she absolutely adored Elvis. So, the guest wanted to do something related to Elvis.

At first I thought maybe they'd have an impersonator sing to her, or maybe even jump out of the cake, but it went even further than that! "I'd like to see if there's an Elvis impersonator who will take her for a ride on Las Vegas Boulevard on a Harley Davidson," he said.

"Oh my," I replied, chuckling. "Well, I'll definitely see what I can do." I was thinking, *I hope you checked this out with Mom first!*

I got everything set up, and I can still remember the woman's face when she came outside and saw Elvis Presley sitting on a Harley, gesturing for her to join him. She was so precious and such a sweet lady! I thought, *she's not going to have the heart for this.*

Still, her family helped get her situated on the bike and strapped a helmet on her. She held on tight to Elvis and there they went! I was really nervous at this point because I thought she'd be upset or shaken when they got back. To my surprise, the very moment they returned the woman took off the helmet, looked around, and let a devious smile spread over her face.

"Let's go again," she said!

Winning the Pot

Heartfelt Moments

Sometimes, concierges are blessed enough to build wonderful relationships with the families and individuals they serve. Other times, they're trusted enough to be allowed to share in some wonderful moments. As with any other job dealing with people, building bonds and attachments is easy. As you can imagine, these concierges might be subjected to a whole range of different emotions... and most of them wouldn't change it for the world!

Friend of the Family

There have been many funny moments in my concierge career, but the most memorable have been the ones that allowed me to form close and meaningful relationships with some of my regular guests. There's a particular family that means a lot to me. They began coming to our hotel in the mid 1990's, when their daughter was just 9 years old. She was quite a character; always wanting to do the craziest things and try whatever looked fun.

The family returned every year, so I really had the chance to get close with them; they asked for me specifically whenever they were visiting. Tragically, at the age of 17, the girl was diagnosed with cancer. It was a total shock to me, and especially to her family. They continued to visit, because Vegas was her favorite place, but she was often unable to attend planned outings at the last minute due to some effect of the chemotherapy.

It was extremely hard to watch her suffer; this girl who had been so completely filled with life prior to her illness. Through it all, I never ceased to be amazed by her strength and her courage. A few years later, she finally beat her cancer down into remission. Joyous isn't the word to describe how I felt about this news! They eventually visited the hotel again, this time with her family and a good friend.

At this point, she was getting ready to celebrate her 21st birthday and her spunk had returned 10-fold. She wanted to go with her friend to celebrate her birthday and her protective father had finally agreed to allow them to go on their own. However, the daughter wanted to visit one of the saucier nightclubs and asked me to arrange the outing without telling her dad. I was put between a rock and a hard spot here, because if anything were to go wrong, it would be my responsibility.

However, as a concierge, there are some situations that need to be nimbly handled. Without telling the daughter or her friend, I discreetly let the parents in on the little secret and got them to stay quiet about it. Therefore, the daughter had a wonderful time and the parents were in on it so they weren't quite as worried. They trusted my judgment enough that they let the girls come to Vegas the next year on their own!

A Special Day at the Zoo

When I plan a day out or make arrangements for a show, it's always important to me that my guests have a wonderful time. I'm sure they always anticipate a great time as well, but to most of us, a day out is just another link in a long chain of memories. On one particular occasion, I was asked to plan an outing that was so much more than that. A colleague of mine was staying at the hotel with a very good friend of his.

This friend had been diagnosed with terminal brain cancer, and my colleague was very stressed out. He wanted to make it very special, and he confided in me that this would likely be the last trip his friend took in her life. She was scheduled for some very aggressive chemotherapy that her doctors didn't expect to make much of a difference. They only expected her to have a few more months of precious life.

As you might imagine, when I learned this, it suddenly turned into the most important moment of my career. Here I was, asked to plan what was probably going to be the last joyous thing this young woman would remember. I found out that she had a very soft spot toward animals, and I had some contacts with the local zoo. I knew that some baby orangutans had just been born about a month prior. I called the director of services and explained the whole situation. His immediate willingness to help was touching. He said he'd meet them at the gate, give them a private tour, and make sure they got some one-on-one time with the baby animals.

One of our hotel cars drove them to the zoo, and they spent the day there. When they returned, the woman's face was just beaming.

She was smiling from ear to ear, and there was pure joy on her face. She came right up to me, gave me a huge hug and kiss, and says, "You just won't believe what we saw."

For the next few minutes, she gushed about the fun they'd had. They'd held and played with the baby orangutans. "They even played ball with me," she said excitedly. She showed me pictures of her and the animals and then she looked at me and said, "I can't explain to you what this means to me." Now, my colleague did not tell her that I knew about her condition, because she didn't want anyone to know. But she was standing there with tears in her eyes, and I was fighting to keep them out of mine. I said, "I'm so happy! We just wanted to make sure you had a great time and could tell your friends how nice your stay was."

The woman passed away a few months after that, but I'll never forget the look on her face when she returned from the zoo. It's very special to me that I was able to help give her that beautiful memory before she passed.

Supporting the Troops

I've handled a lot of wedding arrangements for guests, and I've heard a lot of very touching wedding stories from my fellow concierges – but the one that is most moving for me happened over a July 4th weekend in Vegas. I learned of the request from talking to the mother of a soldier.

"My daughter and her fiancé are both in the service, and they are both currently serving in Iraq. They are in two separate parts of the country, and while my daughter is relatively safe where she is stationed, her fiancé is on the front lines." I expressed my sympathy and asked how I could help. "They are going to be on leave this summer," she said, "and they want to be married in Las Vegas, in your hotel. They need to buy rings and flowers, rent tuxes, everything because they won't have it with them. Also, it is important to them that they not be married in a chapel. Is that something you can arrange?"

Now, before I'd become a concierge, I'd worked as a flight attendant at a small charter airline. We transported American troops to and from the war in Iraq. It might not have been a very important job to some people, but I took it very seriously. It allowed me to do some small part to take care of our soldiers – the men and women who fought for us daily. So, when I heard this story, it instantly became very close to my heart, and it was important for me to help.

I went back and forth on the phone with the mother, trying to pin down an exact date, but it was very difficult because no one knew precisely when the leave was going to happen, and when the couple would arrive. In addition to this, the couple was a young military couple; they didn't have a lot of money to spend on the wedding. So, while we waited to confirm the exact date, I made plans.

The first bit of luck came to me from our hotel. There was a fabulous area on the 32nd floor that was a seating area, with a gorgeous view of the Strip. It was absolutely perfect for a small wedding of 10 to 15. When I found out I could reserve it for free, I was thrilled! As I made the plans, everyone else's patriotic spirit soared – they'd hear about the couple and want to do something for them. Our hotel bakery agreed to make this couple a beautiful cake, for free as well. I found an officiator who wanted to marry the couple on his own time. I was even able to get a few restaurants to agree to feed the guests and wedding party for just $25 a plate – a fabulous price for these outstanding Vegas restaurants.

So, I maintained contact with the mother, and we finally had everything ready – and we'd found out when the couple would arrive. The family and friends met the couple at the airport, and the girlfriend was bawling her eyes out. Her fiancé, who was a big and tough marine, was teary-eyed. It was an extremely touching moment. Knowing they'd spent 35 hours on a plane, I sent the couple to their room in the hotel, where champagne and relaxation awaited them.

The wedding the next day was gorgeous, and went off without a hitch. The hardest part was keeping the bride from ruining her make-up with tears! The couple was so touched at all I'd done for them. However, the light mood was darkened when they found out their leave had been cut short and they had to depart the next day. I thought, *No! You've got to be joking. This poor couple.*

I'll admit, concierges can do a lot of things, but directing the military is a bit beyond our control. Still, I thought, I've got to try and do something. So, I called Fort Worth in North Carolina, thinking that I could explain the situation to someone. I did – several times and to several different people. I kept getting directed here and there, and spoke to so many people. I was really starting to lose hope. Finally, I spoke to a 2-star general and I told him the story and who I was. To my intense surprise, he said, "Your name is Greg? Is this Greg C., the flight attendant on the plane when I was returning from Iraq?"

I couldn't believe it! "Yes! Yes, it is," I said. The general listened to the story and told me he'd see what he could do. Not only was he able to get this couple's leave extended for 3 more days, but he paid for their room for those days! I was ecstatic, and I'd been making these calls without the couples' knowledge, so when I went to them and told them what had happened, and I showed them the e-mail confirmation, they were both in tears. They couldn't believe it. I said, "This is just something small I can do for you... after everything you do for us and this country." I was so overwhelmed. I still get holiday cards and surprise gifts from this couple in the mail, and I'm so thankful I was able to be a part of their lives and do what I did for them.

Revising the Scorecard

One of my most memorable guests was a young man who was dying of cancer. He called me up and asked me to help him plan out his Vegas vacation with his family. He believed this would be the last vacation he ever experienced, and he wanted it to be a memorable time; a way to say 'thank you' and 'goodbye' to his family. I was very touched and honored to be a part of such a significant and special time for him.

He adored golf, and so I made arrangements for him to play on one of the best courses in Vegas. I planned outings and activities that he could do with his family, so that they could spend every available minute together. Everything went very smoothly and he and his family had a wonderful time, despite the bittersweet feeling of the situation. For a long time after the family had gone, I found myself thinking of them and wondering how they were and what had become of them. The young man had been so sweet and appreciative and I often thought of him fondly.

About a year after their visit, I got a phone call from the young man. I answered the phone and he exclaimed, "I lived, Mary! I lived." I burst into tears. I was so happy that it was difficult for me to speak on the phone. He has returned to the hotel since then, and has become a part of many different charities and is quite the activist for cancer research. I know that this young man was able to live for a reason, and I still get goose bumps sharing that story.

A Hawaiian Friend

A gentleman had repeatedly tried to reach one of our hotel guests by phone, but the guest was not picking up. As messages left on the room's voice mail went unanswered and daylight hours turned into night, the friend became increasingly concerned.

Complicating the situation was the fact that this guest was an older Japanese gentleman who spoke no English. He and his wife were visiting from Japan, while their friend was calling from Hawaii to make sure everything was good.

I finally sent a security officer up to the guests' room and, sure enough, they immediately answered the door. They hadn't been picking up the phone for fear that the caller could only speak English. What they failed to realize was that Las Vegas hotels have various people on staff who speak all sorts of foreign languages, and that in this case, I myself happened to be fluent in Japanese.

Security put them on the phone and they were elated to be able to converse with me in their native language. The joy in the Japanese man's voice when I connected him with his friend in Hawaii was palpable; he obviously had not expected to get a call from this dear friend.

Following the conversation, the Japanese couple came down to the front desk in tears. The husband thanked me profusely and handed me a $20 tip, an especially meaningful gesture given the fact that such gratuities are not customary in Japan.

A Lifelong Journey

Just recently I had an elderly guest who was so brittle he could barely stand. He had wisely rented an electronic scooter to help him get around town. One day he pulled up to my desk, rose from his scooter, and pulled a crinkled piece of paper from his pocket.

He put the paper on my desk and slowly and carefully smoothed it out. It became immediately clear that his vision had also weakened with age, as he'd pulled out a flashlight and a magnifying glass. With one hand he held the flashlight, and with the other the magnifying glass, then he stooped over the paper and started to read its contents aloud.

It took me a moment to realize he was reading his boarding pass information. He wanted me to check him in and print out his boarding pass. Naturally we had a line, and everyone was standing on their toes and leaning in close to see and hear what this colorful old gentleman was doing.

Normally I would take a client's information, enter it from the paper, and print their boarding pass quickly. But I couldn't bring myself to interrupt this stately old man, who clearly took great pride in the fact that he could still handle his business. He was so charming and endearing that not a single person in line complained or even sighed as he carefully relayed the information. In fact, many of us had to stifle a chuckle as he refolded the paper, gathered his tools, and returned everything to his trouser pockets.

As I printed his boarding pass, I found myself hoping that when I am his age, I have just as much spunk and self-confidence!

A Sweet Surprise

Many years ago, a couple was married in our hotel. They were so pleased with their ceremony that they came to the hotel every year after, and kept in touch with me. A few years after their marriage, I knew they had just had twins and would be bringing them for their first vacation. Wanting to do something special, I went to the hotel kitchen and ordered a little surprise for them.

To the little boy went a strawberry covered in a white chocolate tuxedo design, and to the little girl went another chocolate-covered strawberry, bearing the design of earrings and a necklace. It was such a small gesture, but the couple was really touched. They visited every year after, and each year, we'd create a new little his and her design for the twins. As little children, they received animals and other amusing designs, and as teenagers, they got credit card strawberries and CD player ones. The family has gone so far as to put together an album with all the different designs we've come up with over the years.

I thought it was so charming how they got to witness a new design every year, and each year we were able to see the twins growing!

Moscow on the Strip

A large group of Russian tourists booked a block of suites in the hotel. They ended up changing their time of departure to ensure that everyone could go home on the same plane, but they neglected to tell one member of their party.

As this particular teenage girl was enjoying some time at the spa, the rest of her party checked out and somehow failed to realize that she was missing! When the girl went back to her room, she was not only locked out but also suddenly very terrified as she spoke not a word of English. By that time, her group had boarded their plane and was on their way back to the Motherland.

I was so upset for her that I even ended up calling my own husband and saying to him, "Can you imagine?" If that had been me at a young age – a girl left behind in another country – I would have been terrified! Since another huge group of guests was coming into the hotel that night, I didn't have a room I could put the girl in. Instead, through a co-worker, I explained that she could come home with me until new travel arrangements were made.

Even though the Russian teenager and I spoke two different languages, we got along famously. I made her dinner, took her for a walk around the neighborhood and laughed as we both tried to explain things to each other by pointing and gesturing. We had a lot of fun, and I was surprised to find that despite the language barrier I had made a new friend.

Though my guest was only supposed to stay with me that first night, it ultimately took three days for us to book her on a new flight to Russia. After this unexpected little adventure, my husband started to tease me at dinner every night, asking "Who are you bringing home tomorrow?"

I still get Christmas cards from my Russian friend, even though it's been many years now since her extended stay. The trip to Vegas was the only time she ever traveled to the U.S. and each year, she signs her holiday card with the same funny greeting – "Wishing I was (still) there."

Lost and Bound

It's not all fun and games in Las Vegas. In a town where the highest of highs coexist with the lowest of lows, there's a kind of odd, super-charged atmosphere that can sometimes tip people in the wrong direction.

For example, we had a pair of newlyweds who had been drinking and gambling all evening. The combination of too much excitement and too little sleep obviously started to wear on them, because that night they had their first fight as a married couple, one that began loudly in the lobby.

When they went up to their room, the wife suddenly realized that she had left her new wedding ring in the casino beside one of the slots. She came rushing down to the concierge desk to ask for help and thankfully, we were able to quickly locate her ring.

However, there were evidently deeper issues at play with the young couple. When the wife went back upstairs, she caught her husband in the act of trying to hang himself by his belt in the bathroom! Hard to believe, but true.

The woman ran screaming into the hall and fortunately, a security guard happened to be passing by at just that moment. He rushed into the bathroom and cut her husband loose. Normally, we would have to file a police report for this kind of event, but after much convincing by the wife, we agreed to record it as an internal hotel security matter only.

The next morning at checkout, the husband was extremely subdued. To this day, I still feel the twinge of a nasty flashback whenever a guest comes to the concierge desk to tell me that they've misplaced valuables in the casino.

The High Stakes of Life

Unfortunately, accidents do happen while guests are staying in Vegas, and sometimes, those accidents are very serious. There have been a few times that I've had to comfort guests and help make arrangements that were not celebratory or happy at all. For instance, one of my guests had a heart attack, and he and his wife were here from another country. Neither of them spoke the language, and I accompanied his wife to the hospital and comforted her throughout the ordeal.

Another time, one of my guests passed away during his stay. He was an older gentleman and I gathered all of his belongings and organized them so that I could ship them home. His wife received them, and not long after, she paid me a personal visit. She thanked me for doing what I did, and her eyes filled with tears. She was from another country as well and wouldn't have been able to make it to Vegas in order to gather her husband's items. She was touched by what she called my 'kindness.' I told her that her husband had been my guest, and that it had been my pleasure to help in any way I could.

Thank goodness this is not usually the kind of 'loss' we're accustomed to dealing with in Vegas, but when it happens, the family needs someone there who can think calmly and help make arrangements. As a concierge, service sometimes transcends worldly bounds.

Buttering Up Some Guests

One of my Las Vegas patrons, Frank, is someone that I previously worked with at another hotel in Florida for a number of years before I moved to Nevada. But you would never guess how innocently the relationship with him and his family began.

They were getting ready to watch a movie in their hotel room and wanted to eat some freshly popped popcorn while doing so. At this particular Florida hotel, there was no in-room dining, but we did have an old fashioned popcorn machine in the lobby, which I used to make them some delicious popcorn.

About three months later, a Ferrari pulled up to front of the hotel and out gets Frank and his son. I am floored, as these people were always totally down to earth and you would never have guessed that they were so well-to-do. Turns out Frank is the CEO of a major corporation and has a large collection of sports cars.

From that point on, they became regular guests of mine for six years, and we formed such a strong relationship that when their son, Michael, grew older, he chose to attend a local university near the Florida hotel. We promised to keep in touch and sure enough, here in Las Vegas, although he stays at a different hotel, he always stops by to say hi.

Kermit the Frog

I was handling a wedding for a woman whose father was setting it all up. She was Daddy's little girl, and her father absolutely adored her. We were handling everything from the bachelor and bachelorette parties to the reception, etc.

One day we were talking and the bride was reminiscing about her childhood. One of the stories she mentioned was about her singing the 'Rainbow Connection' to her dad when she was little. As she told the story, her dad got a little misty-eyed, and I could tell that this was a very special memory between the two of them.

Remembering that story, I bought a 'Kermit Frog' and wrapped it up. I gave it to the bride and told her to give it to her dad as a gift on the wedding night. Neither of them was expecting it, as neither knew what the gift was. When he opened it, they both were so touched! It was a small gesture I could do that meant so much to both of them, and it was really beautiful.

Paying the Runner

Famous Faces

One of the coolest things about being a concierge in Vegas is having the opportunity to meet some of the most famous people in the world. Sometimes, it can be awkward or funny, because as a concierge, you're allowed just a few steps into these people's private worlds. Famous people often have the most outlandish requests of a concierge, and as you're about to see, the results can end up miraculous, or very uncomfortable.

Private Concert

There are two things the general public may not know about a certain Motown crooner. The first is that he never books his Vegas hotel rooms in advance, and the other is that he has a phenomenal memory. It was a Valentine's Day weekend and our hotel was packed. I received a phone call from a man who identified himself as the bodyguard of one of the most accomplished musicians of all time. "We're en route to your hotel and we're going to need a two-bedroom suite," he said, and then he hung up.

I thought, *is this guy for real or am I being the butt-end of a joke, here?* Still, I didn't want to take any chances so I sped over to the front desk and asked if we had any two-bedroom suites. I was told no, and so I asked if we had any reservations that were vacant at the moment. Thankfully, we did. I said, "I'll personally walk that guest to another hotel, but this certain musician is coming and we're going to check him into this suite."

I went out front to wait for his arrival, and after about half an hour, a limousine pulls in and out steps a legend. I had met this man only one other time, 15 years prior, at another hotel in Petaluma, California. After I'd introduced myself and welcomed him, I asked what the occasion was, and why he was in town. He joked, "Well if you can't pet a luma, what can you pet?" So, as I watched him step out of the limo in Vegas, I chuckled at the memory. Then, I walked over and introduced myself again. I said, "I had the pleasure of meeting you about 15 years ago at another hotel."

He replied, "Yes. I remember. I was doing a concert in Petaluma and I joked that if you can't pet a luma, what could you pet?" Well, this particular musical genius happens to be blind, so you can imagine how blown away I was. He had remembered my voice and my name after all that time. I took him to his suite and made sure he was comfortable. His bodyguard told me that they'd like to come down in about an hour and have dinner.

When they came down for dinner, it just so happened that we had a piano player providing the dinner music. My musical guest seemed to be enjoying the melody. His head was swaying back and forth, and he was smiling. After his dinner, he said to me, "Would that happen to be Carlos P. playing the piano?" He was our regular piano player, and I replied, "As a matter of fact, it is." And my guest said, "Would you go over and ask if I could join him on the piano. Please tell him who I am and remind him that he and I played a concert in Germany." I said, "Of course," and so I went over and repeated the message to the piano player.

The piano player was thrilled. "Yes, of course. Please tell him to come in. I haven't seen him since Germany." So I guided my guest over toward the piano. The dining room was absolutely loaded with lovers celebrating Valentine's Day, and when our guest sat down at the piano, suddenly, there was a thundering applause and people were whistling and shouting. The other guests were completely enamored, and our musician played sweet love songs for about an hour and a half. I'd be willing to bet there wasn't one guest who got up during that time and walked out. It was completely impromptu, and it was one of the most beautiful concerts I've had the pleasure of witnessing.

A Friendly Giant

By the time this famous blue-eyed singer reached his 77th birthday, he had experienced the ups and downs of a remarkable career as well as established a reputation for having a volatile, two-sided personality. When he was nice, he was very nice, but when he got into a fit about someone or something, it could be very ugly, earning him the nickname, 'The Chairman.' Thankfully, I got to glimpse his nicer side.

As The Chairman was getting ready to head back to his Vegas penthouse suite after a show, an elderly woman started walking alongside him and his phalanx of bodyguards. When the group got to the front door of his deluxe, private area, one of the bodyguards brushed her aside as he opened the door for his boss. But that did not sit well at all with the guest of honor.

He pushed his bodyguard out of the way, took the elderly woman by the hand and gently led her back to the elevator, where he pressed the down button and made sure that she got safely back on the elevator. He then sternly instructed his bodyguard to never treat a woman like that again.

On another occasion, The Chairman got wind that a pair of newlyweds fans were coming to the show that night. At the twilight stage of his career, this iconic star always got an extra big kick out of his younger fans, especially ones like these who professed to have all his albums.

This arranged for the brand new couple to be seated in the front row with a complimentary bottle of champagne and at the end of the show, took out his pocket hankie and gave it to them as a me-

mento. As you might expect, the young couple couldn't stop raving the next day about the special treatment they had received.

But the "piece de resistance" was the time this entertainer read a front-page Las Vegas newspaper story about a family with a disabled daughter whose special van had been stolen. Just like that, he decided he was going to buy the family a new, replacement vehicle even though he had never met or seen them before.

The Chairman wrote a check of just under $100,000 for the specially equipped replacement van and insisted that his identity be kept secret. It was a kindness I will never forget, and one I suspect I'm not likely to see again anytime soon.

Saddling Up for the Rodeo

Early on during my concierge career, I was working at a rundown and since demolished Las Vegas property where the carpets were faded, the lighting poor and the paint cracked. Still, I did my best to provide five-star concierge assistance to the guests.

During the National Rodeo Finals held every year in December, one of the event's famous performers called up ahead of time with a most unusual request, even for Vegas. "I need a room and I need something big enough so that I can bring my horse," he said. I tried to explain our "No Pets" policy, but the rodeo star was adamant.

"My horse *has* to be with me," he insisted. "Don't you have a villa or something like that, where there would be enough room for both of us?"

In the beginning I thought this guy was having a go at me, but I quickly realized he was very serious. I decided I would do whatever I could to make this cowboy happy. I went all the way up to the hotel chain president and was finally allowed to reserve a bungalow at the very back of the hotel complex for the rodeo star and his ride.

The weekend of the big rodeo finally arrived and our eccentric cowboy walked into the lobby. We had been preparing for days to house a live animal, but when he arrived, I was in complete shock. He was NOT accompanied by a real live horse, but a life-sized mock-up that the cowboy was reluctant to store elsewhere for fear it might get damaged. All at once, I was embarrassed, relieved, and worried that my boss might possibly hog-tie me!

The cowboy hadn't lied: he did check in with an oversized equestrian companion. But for better or worse, our kitchen never did have to deal with room service orders of buckets of oats and carrots.

Trick Play

A professional football player came to me asking for help with a popular Las Vegas play. He was flying his girlfriend into town and wanted to propose at the hotel. "I'm good at a lot of things," he boasted, "but I'm not exactly a hopeless romantic. Can you please help me?"

We quickly went to work. At the hotel coffee shop, I helped him brainstorm a romantic love note, which I wrote up on very nice, expensive stationary and placed in the bedroom of their hotel suite, with a trail of rose petals for added effect. I also got Mr. Wide Receiver to agree to the idea of placing the ring at the bottom of a champagne glass, to be filled and served to her in the room.

Everything went according to plan and the girlfriend said yes, but soon after the athlete shared a residual concern. It was the handwritten love note that had really sold his girlfriend and he was now concerned about recreating that kind of poetry in the future. "You've created a monster!" he teased. Then, turning deadly serious, he added: "We're going to have to tell her the truth."

To the NFL superstar's credit, he went ahead that very same day and confessed that the love note was almost all my doing. Instead of getting angry, the bride-to-be actually got a kick out of the whole thing! She knew it took a lot of courage to both have asked for help in the first place and then be willing to reveal the maneuver to her.

I am happy to report that as of this year, this couple is still very happily married.

The Politics of Lunch

The Speaker of the House came to our hotel restaurant for lunch. It was a big deal, and the Secret Service was everywhere.

When the Speaker's car pulled up to the front of the hotel, a gaggle of burly-looking security guys jumped out first – to make sure the area was 'secure,' I suppose. Then, the Speaker himself was ushered from the back of the car into the hotel.

After the driver of that particular car closed the passenger door and walked back around to the driver's side to get in and wait, he discovered that the car was now locked and the keys were sitting in the ignition. He immediately panicked, because this is not exactly the kind of run-of-the-mill vehicle that can be cracked with a coat hanger.

As the luncheon went on, hoards of Secret Servicemen were buzzing through the hotel lobby and outside, like bees in a garden. I wondered what our other guests were thinking; that perhaps there had been a bomb threat or that someone's life was in danger. Apparently, it didn't attract too much attention, because no one asked.

It took half an hour for the car to be re-opened, they finally managed. For a few weeks after that, the joke around the hotel was, "How many Secret Servicemen does it take to unlock a car door?"

Groupie Alert

One day I found myself in the presence of a particularly devoted Jon Bon Jovi fan.

She was a bubbly trophy wife who, in matter of just a few minutes at check-in, started going on and on about how much she loved the New Jersey lead singer, all the concerts she had seen and how desperate she was to get tickets for one of the band's sold-out Las Vegas performances that weekend.

While the woman was chatting away, I noticed her husband standing by her side very quietly. He wore coke-bottle glasses and a dowdy haircut – probably the total opposite of Jon Bon Jovi – and I could tell that her enthusiasm was making him uncomfortable. As you can imagine, I felt empathetic toward the man, and as the wife kept talking, I began to share his discomfort.

I reached across the desk and gently touched the wife's hand. "You don't need to worry about seeing Jon Bon Jovi this weekend," I told her. "Not when you've got such a good-looking husband by your side. How about making this weekend a Jon Bon Jovi-free experience?"

Immediately, the woman stopped her incessant chatter about the rock star, and her husband gave a tiny laugh. And you know what? I never did hear her mention Jon Bon Jovi's name again. I guess you could say she stopped giving love a bad name.

Lights, Camera, Friction!

A number of big-budget movies are filmed in Las Vegas and when that happens, our hotel is sometimes a temporary home for cast and crew, not to mention tons of paparazzi and fans hoping to catch a glimpse of the stars.

To guard against this fan and media crush, various precautions are put in place. One of the most common is to book the big leads of a major motion picture in accommodations that are off the Strip, so that these people do not have to walk through a crowded, open lobby.

In one such case, a leading man in one such movie caused us headaches by never actually spending any time at his off-the-Strip rental. Instead, he strayed to all places except his comfy, private Vegas digs. Through it all, his wife called obsessively. At first, we simply said that we couldn't locate him, but as it became obvious that the cheating A-lister was never going to be in his villa, it became more difficult for us to cover for him.

Our 'guest' and his handlers instructed us to hold all calls from his wife. His wife meanwhile would constantly try her husband's cell phone and then get on the horn to us, furious that we could not locate him at the villa. The wife I think eventually got wise to the whole situation and stopped calling the front desk and my concierge desk. A few months later, sure enough, the celebrity news mags had front page stories about Mr. Movie Star's ugly impending divorce.

The Show Must Go On

We had an extremely popular rock band staying at the hotel. Imagine our surprise when one of the staffers found the lead singer passed out on a landing beside the elevators.

A colleague and I rushed to his side and immediately began performing CPR. When I couldn't find a pulse, I really began to freak out. The paramedics soon arrived and whipped out a huge syringe full of adrenaline. Without warning, one of the EMT folks jabbed the needle straight into the rock star's chest, just like that scene in Pulp Fiction or any number of other Hollywood movies. It was surreal.

Moments later, the formerly comatose rocker sat straight up and mumbled, "What the hell is going on here!?" The paramedics loaded him onto a stretcher and took him to the hospital for further observation, while everyone at the front desk assumed the big Las Vegas concert that night was off.

A few hours later, the very same rock star waltzed back through the lobby as if nothing had happened and headed up to his suite. Apparently, he was not going to let something as trivial as a drug induced coma get in the way of a good show. Eight hours after lying motionless by a bank of elevators, he was on stage in front of thousands of concertgoers, bellowing out hit songs. File this under sex, drugs and... hard to believe.

Car Crash

A famous, Italian-born Formula 1 race car driver was staying at our hotel. Tragically, he was involved in a terrible car accident on the streets of Las Vegas. With severe injuries, he was airlifted to the nearest hospital. One of his legs was badly mangled, but doctors were able to operate right away and save it.

In the meantime, this poor man's wife was back in Europe in a frenzy. She spoke only Italian, and when she tried to call the hospital, she was unable to get any information at all. I can't imagine how scared she must have been. Luckily, I speak the language and within a few hours of learning about the situation, was able to start giving her regular updates.

She flew into town to be with her husband, and I ended up becoming very close with her during this difficult time. After the operation, the race car driver stayed for a few more weeks at our hotel, until he was able to travel. Although the circumstances were very scary and trying, his wife ended up recommending our hotel to many of her well-heeled European friends. She was so happy with the work I'd done, and couldn't stop thanking me. They return to the hotel often, and I like to think of them as great friends. Strangely enough, even accidents like this have a silver lining.

The Movie Star Workout

I had the pleasure of catering to one of Hollywood's all-time greatest actors, who just so happened to be a beautiful humanitarian and founder of a particular food company. For privacy reasons, this man liked to very cleverly exercise by walking up and down the stairwells in the hotels he stayed in. Every morning after breakfast, he would ascend and descend from floor to floor in the company of a good friend with whom he liked to travel.

The friend alerted me to this habit in advance, so security wouldn't become alarmed at the sight of two older gentlemen going up and down the stairs. Armed with this information, I put some notes of encouragement in the stairwell, along with water bottles and towels, all at strategic intervals. My famous guest loved it!

For the duration of his stay, he kept telling everyone how delightful he thought the whole thing was. At the end of his stay, he gifted me with a case of very expensive wine as a thank you. This lovely star passed away a couple of years ago, and although I'm sure he'd experienced every level of luxury throughout his years, my stairwell stunt spoke to him. He stayed with us again before his death, and all he could talk about was what might be waiting for him in the stairwell this time!

What are the Odds?

Funny: Ha Ha!

Perhaps one of the greatest challenges is keeping it together for guests when all you want to do is giggle until you cry. There are many times when a guest will do or say something very hilarious, but a concierge wouldn't dare laugh at someone they were serving. Of course, there are times when the guests and the concierge share a chuckle, but those times when a concierge shouldn't laugh can often be the funniest!

Morning Glory

At one point in my career, I was working the overnight shift at a small Las Vegas boutique hotel, where they wanted a concierge on duty at all hours. It was just myself and a desk clerk. One night, around 2am, we suddenly heard a loud male voice coming from the direction of the elevators.

"Help! Can someone please help me?" The voice was so loud and urgent that my colleague and I both had the same thought: call security! At that moment, a wrinkled and completely naked older man walked into the main lobby area. His hands were covering his privates, and he had a sheepish look on his face. Quickly, I grabbed a couple of pillows from the lobby couch and handed them to the elderly guest, who gladly accepted them as a temporary form of cover for his front and behind!

"Sir, what's the matter?" I asked, trying to figure out what in the world would have this man in the lobby at 2am without a single stitch of clothing. After a long pause, where the man looked anywhere but at me, he replied, "My girlfriend kicked me out of the room."

Although it was quite humorous, I was able to keep from laughing until we got security to let the man back into his room. I didn't think my poor guest would join in my mirth.

Cloudy with a Chance of Mirth

One thing that never fails to surprise me is the amounts of information guests expect concierges to know. Of course, most Vegas visitors are distracted with everything there is to see and do, but nevertheless it can be quite funny. Most guests can pretty much tell what the weather is going to be like by peering out their window, or turning on the local news. Still, they'll call down to the concierge desk to ask how hot it is or how hot it's going to be later in the evening.

A colleague of mine decided to have a little fun on his last day before moving on to another job. We had a young, bubbly guest who'd been taking in the hottest Vegas shows and soaking up the sun's rays by the pool each day. When she called down to check the weather, my co-worker said, "Please hold one minute, Ma'am, while I check with our staff meteorologist."

After a little pause and a bit of giggling, my co-worker got back on the phone and let the guest know how warm it was going to be. It was all harmless, of course, but a few days later when the same woman called down to get the day's weather from the 'hotel meteorologist,' the concierge on duty was more than a little baffled!

Background Action

I had just begun working as a Las Vegas concierge when an episode of a major TV drama began filming on site at the hotel. In addition to programs like Vegas that are set on the Strip, many other shows come to town at one point or another to shoot a Strip-themed special episode. It's often the case that the director makes use of the hotel staff as extras. It was a very exciting and new experience for me and I greatly enjoyed pretending to do my job on camera and silently mouthing conversations with customers in the background.

Toward the end of the day, one of the actors was set to play the part of a female concierge for a scene. However, the show's wardrobe department didn't have a proper uniform. Instead, they asked me for my concierge uniform, and by asked, I mean they pretty much said, "Hand it over, sweetheart." Willing to sacrifice for the greater good of dramatic television, I did.

The producers still wanted me to help out with the background action for that scene, but the only thing available was a janitor's uniform! There's no arguing with TV big shots, so before long I was cleaning up in the background in my janitor's uniform. I still wonder if any hardcore fans have noticed that the same person who was a concierge in one shot was a janitor in another.

The Accidental Threesome

A hotel guest lingered around my desk one afternoon before approaching me to get directions to the Grand Canyon. However, he lingered a bit, and his eyes kept darting around, and soon it became clear that he wanted to discuss something else entirely. A few moments after I'd given him the run-down on how to get to the Grand Canyon, he leaned forward and whispered, "I've got to tell you something."

I immediately became worried, because you just never know what a guest might say to you in any given moment.

"I'm very upset with your housekeeping department," he continued quietly. "We had a 'Do Not Disturb' sign on our door, but I'm afraid the maid came in anyway." I immediately assured the young man that our housekeeper was very good about following proper procedure before entering. "Oh, she knocked," he admitted, starting to blush, "but when we didn't answer, she unlocked the door and walked in."

Puzzled, I was wondering why he didn't answer the door. That's when he leaned a little further toward me and said, "I was right in the middle of making love to my wife... and at exactly THAT moment, the maid showed up and I'm afraid we just couldn't stop." He looked so pained as he explained this last part that it was all I could do to keep from giggling. Instead, I replied, "Sir, I'm so sorry that happened to you. Do you want me to call the manager so you can make an official complaint?"

"Absolutely not," the young man scoffed, apparently horrified with the idea of having to relate the story to anyone else. "I am just very, very upset and I wanted you to know about this." I patiently thanked him for bringing the matter to my attention, but neglected to tell him that most of the staff already knew about this unfortunate episode of coitus interruptus, thanks to a very talkative and still-smiling maid.

Honeymoon Surprise

Back when I first became a Las Vegas concierge, I was assigned my first room set-up after a couple of weeks on the job.

The room in question was one of our deluxe honeymoon suites and my job was to prepare it for a newlywed couple arriving later on that day. However, there was a lack of communication from the front desk, because as I was busy arranging candles, rose petals, lotions, a massage table and more, the newly minted husband and wife checked in early and made their way upstairs.

I was nearly startled to death when the door burst open and the groom walked in carrying his bride across the threshold. Luckily, because it was a suite, I happened to be in one of the adjoining rooms. Not knowing what to do, I hid behind a door, panicked about what to do next. What could I do? I thought perhaps I should clear my throat and walk out of the adjoining room, but what if the husband and wife were in the middle of a romantic moment? The embarrassment I faced was almost too horrible to think about!

The thought even crossed my mind that I might stay hidden and wait until the couple left the hotel room – but I had no idea how long that might take and eventually, my boss and co-workers would start to wonder where I'd gone. Then, there was the obvious issue of the couple's privacy. I knew I had to get out of there soon, and I was about to do the unthinkable.

However, the young couple decided to take in the sumptuous balcony view, affording me the chance to sneak out of the room before being detected. I would have hated to spoil their special moment, but I took a lot of ribbing from my colleagues over the whole thing. They teased me for days about now knowing what it felt like to be the "other woman."

Truth or Dare

One week, we had a large family stay at our hotel. Among their brood was an unusually talkative and outgoing eight-year-old boy, Todd, with whom I would have these very animated conversations. The family was very outgoing, and we joked quite often. On the final day of their stay, I was working in the concierge lounge overseeing our continental breakfast when the family came in for their final meal at the hotel.

After they'd been seated for a few minutes, I heard them laughing loudly and looked over to see what the commotion was. They were nudging Todd in my direction, but uncharacteristically, he was acting very shy. Todd's dad said, loudly enough for me to hear, "I will give you ten dollars if you do it."

Todd blushed and covered his face, then seizing the moment as only today's youth can, peeked out at his dad and countered, "I'll do it for a hundred." Sure enough, the boy's father pulled out a hundred-dollar bill. Todd immediately jumped to his feet, walked over to my desk, got down on one knee and said softly, "Will you marry me?" By that time, the entire breakfast crowd was paying attention, and burst out laughing at the sight of a kid proposing to an adult female concierge.

The family was in hysterics as Todd rushed back to the table to grab his $100 bill. However, I figured he needed to do a little bit more to truly earn his pay. I said, "Todd, you left so quickly that I didn't have a chance to give you an answer. Come here." Sheepishly, Todd walked back over toward me and I said, "The answer is yes. I'll marry you if you ask me again in twenty years." Todd grinned and returned to his table, greeted by high-fives and laughter. The dad was so thrilled by my play-along spirit that I too was rewarded with $100. Shades of what the dad will have to fork out when Todd gets married for real.

Bedroom Shenanigans

A bunch of guys had come to Vegas for a bachelor party and wanted to prank the husband-to-be. The plan was to place a blow-up doll under the sheets in his room before he checked in. I ran to the adult store and bought one, but then when I got back to the hotel, I realized I wouldn't be able to blow the thing up by myself. So, I grabbed the helium tank and blew the doll up in the room.

I tucked it under the sheets, thinking they and the comforter would hold the doll in place for the surprise. I went on about my business without giving it another thought. A few hours later, I got a call from my general manager. He explained to me that a maid with our housekeeping staff had fainted upstairs and was being attended to by paramedics.

"What?" I asked. "Yes," he replied. "Apparently, the maid walked into a room and saw a dead body pressed against the ceiling." The words were so bizarre that it took me a few moments to realize what he meant. The blow-up doll had somehow gotten free of the sheets and had floated up to the ceiling! Although it's humorous now, it's safe to say that my general manager didn't find it very funny. My colleagues still occasionally ask about the day the blow-up doll... blew up in my face.

Gender Bender

I was enlisted, quite innocently I might add, as a co-conspirator when a couple of guys wanted to prank the rest of the group they were staying with. They approached the desk and said they had a special request. "You see, last weekend, the two of us were left out of a boating trip by our buds. The reason was that the boats held only seven people each, but counting the ice chests, only six could fit. Our friends were put to a choice: us or the chests full of beer. We lost," the guest explained. His friend picked up from there and told me the rest of the story.

"Of course, our friends apologized but we are still haunted by the memories. We thought we might give them what they deserved through the legal system, but the death penalty seems a little harsh," he joked. They then explained their plan and how I could help. The group of fourteen men would be looking for something to do that weekend, and the two guests wanted me to suggest a particular nightclub.

Later in the day, I was able to spend a moment with the whole group, and when the topic of the weekend came up, I began discussing the best night clubs. "The very best," I told them, "is this great little place right down the street. The drinks are reasonably priced and if you haven't been, it's a total MUST." The guys asked for the name of the club again, and I knew I'd played my part well.

Friday night, the two pranksters agreed to meet the rest of their entourage at the club, but claimed they had something to do first. A few minutes later, the other twelve gentlemen entered one of the most popular and lively gay bars in Vegas. About ten minutes after that, a group of gay bikers pulled up in front of the bar and joined the crowd. The jig at that point was up, as the bikers were fully duded out in chaps and even had a club name and insignia on their jackets that gave away the true nature of the drinking establishment.

But here's where I have to give the group credit. Instead of bolting at that point and getting angry at having been set up, they refused to leave and go anywhere else on their last night unless the other two joined them for a drink there first. No one in the group "came out" that night, which would have really been the icing on the prank cake. Maybe next year.

Going to Calgary

After his trip to Las Vegas, a guest was scheduled to go back to Hong Kong, and then make another trip to Calgary. He wanted to know how he could get to Calgary from Hong Kong. I asked if he'd like me to find some flight information.

"No," he said. "I want to drive!" Puzzled, I stood there for a moment before he said again, "I want to drive to Calgary." I now realized that the man wasn't thinking about the Pacific Ocean he'd have to drive over, but I didn't want to embarrass him. So, I pulled out a map and showed him the locations.

Seeing this big body of water between his home and his destination seemed to embarrass the guest anyway, and as he walked away, I wondered if there might not have been a better way to tell him. In any case, he never asked for that flight information!

Contact Number

When I first started working as a concierge, I wanted to make sure my guests could reach me if there was an emergency. For this reason, I gave one of my guests my cell phone number. I had been serving this guest for a few days, and was helping with a particularly large project, so I wanted to make sure nothing went wrong.

At two o'clock in the morning, my phone rang. I saw it was from the hotel, so I picked up quickly, hoping nothing was wrong. "I wanted to know if you could get me into this particular club, and also maybe reserve a limo," my guest says.

It took me a moment to respond, because I was still half-asleep. "I'm sorry," I said. "I don't have access to my computer right now. I was actually sleeping and I have to get up very early in the morning."

I had no idea how literally the guest would take it when I told him to 'call if he needed something.' That's when I learned that concierges never give out their personal numbers, because it would be the end of personal time, period!

Tackling the Dancer

It IS Vegas, so when guests become completely inebriated, it's usually not a surprise, and anything that needs to be handled is done with tact by the concierge. Forgotten room keys and other accidents are quite normal. However, one of my guests became very drunk one night during dinner. In fact, I suspect he'd been drinking long before then.

We have a piano player in our dining room, and as most guests were clearing out, he played a jaunty little tune that was very upbeat. Suddenly, my guest jumps up on the table and begins performing a strip tease right there. Of course, there was nothing I could do personally, but I had to get this guest out of there! I called security, and they came as quickly as possible.

I could see the hesitation in the eyes of the three men. In the time it had taken them to arrive, my guest had shed every single piece of his clothing. He was now dancing very unsteadily on the tabletop, knocking dishes over, and he was extremely sweaty and... well, let's just say he had a lot of hair.

The lead security man was an older gentleman, who was very refined and embarrassed quite easily. There was an awkward moment while the three security men looked back and forth at each other. You could almost hear their thoughts. We have to tackle this hairy, drunk, naked guy... as in... physical contact?

But after another moment, they did their job and got my drunken dancer out of our dining room. I'm so thankful it was almost empty, but the few diners who had been present weren't offended. They were laughing and cheering at the security guards, and applauded their efforts!

BUST!

Funny: Peculiar

Many times, a concierge will be called into a situation that leaves them puzzled and confused. Even those who have been around the block or two will experience guests or situations that they wonder about long after their shift has ended for the day! As you'll see in the following stories, what happens in Vegas is sometimes just weird.

Where Amazing Happens

As someone who offers management, concierge, and personal assistant services to people in residences and corporate settings, I've dealt with my fair share of beyond-the-hotel-norm situations. For instance, I once had a gentleman call from a large leased home in a gated Las Vegas community. He complained that the power had been turned off and sure enough, when we arrived, not a single indoor or outdoor light fixture would turn on.

Puzzled, we called the electric company to confirm that the power was up to date. My colleague, just out of sheer curiosity, unscrewed a few light bulbs and gently examined them, shaking them so he could hear. In short order, we realized that every single light bulb in the pace was burnt out! Now, I don't mean twelve or thirteen light bulbs – I mean the lights outside near the garden, the lights by the pool, the overhead lights in every single room – not a single light bulb worked.

We finally deduced how the light bulbs in every single socket of the large home had come to be simultaneously extinguished. The owner of the property as a big NBA star who used the investment residence only sporadically as a starting off point for off-season nightclub expeditions. The athlete and his friends were essentially always coming home from their nights of partying in broad daylight, and had never realized that the lights had been left on. The cycle repeated until evidently, they packed up for another basketball season and left without turning off the switches.

Of course, regular people like you and me would have quickly noticed the electricity bill and put an end to it. But the homeowner's business manager had been dutifully paying the electricity bill for months. We ended up itemizing all the different kinds of light bulbs in the house and made a trip to a hardware store to buy 67 light bulbs in all. Amazing!

TV or Not TV?

Working in some of the most beautiful hotels in Vegas, I was accustomed to guests being a little 'star struck' at some of the amenities in their rooms. However, once I had a woman come down to the concierge desk and let me know she had a problem.

"There's a TV set in my room," she said, with a panicked look on her face. Puzzled, I waited for her to elaborate. "There's a TV set in my room," she repeated. I wondered for a moment if she was joking with me, but it was apparent that she was very serious. "There's a TV in every room," I explained.

"Oh no. I don't want it," she said, shaking her head vigorously. She was an Eastern European woman, older in age, and I wondered if perhaps she was having a problem with the television. Then, she added, "I don't want to pay extra."

Realizing what she thought, I explained that the televisions were amenities, and every guest had one in their room. "So, I can watch for free?" she asked. "Absolutely," I assured her. "The only things you have to pay for are premium channels if you order them, like the pay-per-view movies or adult movies. But even then, you'll be asked several times to confirm that you want to order the program."

She took it all in for a moment, looking surprised that she'd be able to watch the TV without paying extra. Then she said, "What is adult movie?" Blushing a little, I tried to explain. "It's pornography," I said, but she looked clueless. "It means sex movies," I said, my cheeks now completely crimson. Hers matched mine when she realized what I meant. "Oh," she said, wide-eyed. "That's not for me." She stood there a moment longer and then added, "But I do understand it costing extra."

Geography 101

Most guests that come to Vegas hotels are a pleasure to serve. However, as a concierge – as there often are with other people-oriented professions – there are sometimes guests who are rude. I once had three men come to the desk who were Middle Eastern, and from the very beginning they were rude, aggressive and loud. One of them asked me about booking a Grand Canyon tour, and I was explaining the West and South Rim.

However, the guest interrupted me and said, "I want to go as close to the mountains as possible." I said, "I understand, sir," and I explained again about the Skywalk, and how there were nice trails in the South Rim. The man was becoming visibly upset by this point, and he interrupted me again. "I don't know what's so hard for you to understand," he shouted. Other guests and colleagues were looking at us now. "I want to get close to the mountains," he said again, his face turning red.

I was horrified at this point, because it was obvious that the man wanted something, but I wasn't sure what to say. You can only get so close to the 'mountains' and I thought I had covered everything. After having been interrupted and basically called stupid by this man, I'd never been yelled at by a guest before and called stupid. It's safe to say that I was more than a little offended. After taking a deep breath, I tried again.

"Sir, I'm sorry. Is there a different way that I could explain it to you? I'm not quite sure what you're asking for."

Well, now the man was absolutely fit to be tied. Leaning forward, while his companions shook their heads and shifted their weight angrily, the man shouted, "Look. I just want to be as close as possible to the faces of your presidents of the United States!" When I realized what the man was asking for, I no longer felt quite as horrible.

"Sir," I said calmly, "You're asking about tours to the Grand Canyon. The faces of the presidents are at Mount Rushmore in South Dakota." Suddenly, the man froze, realizing that the error had been his, not mine, and looked very embarrassed. Quickly, he said thank you, and left. I thought that perhaps next time, the guest might be a little more patient with the concierge.

C.S.I.: Honeymoon Suite

Our hotel had been open for just a week, so all of the bedding in the rooms was white... *really* white. We had some newlyweds checking in, and two of us went up to a honeymoon suite to prepare it. We placed champagne and chocolate strawberries on the bedside table, and scattered fresh rose petals across the pillows and king-size bed. The effect was beautiful, and I was excited for our newlyweds to see it!

A few hours later, we returned for a final walk-through, as the couple was due to arrive in about half an hour. We were absolutely appalled to find that those white sheets were stained red; it looked like a murder scene! We'd had no idea that the fresh rose petals would do that, and just like a couple of criminals trying to cover up a crime, we scrambled to clean up the mess.

Stripping the sheets, we frantically called down and had housekeeping bring us fresh ones, and picked up all of the rose petals. Also, making a hotel bed isn't the same as making a bed in the average person's home. There's the mattress protector, the bottom sheet, a top sheet, a blanket, and then the duvet – not to mention the pillowcases – and there's a certain process that makes it all look neat and cozy. By the time we'd finished making the bed as quickly as we could, we were both sweating and breathing heavily.

We were walking down the hall, rolling our evidence in a housekeeping cart, as a fellow staff member came out of the elevator, escorting the couple to their room. From that point on, I made sure to put all complimentary roses in table vases!

Slumber Party

In the not-too-distant past, Las Vegas hotel bellmen took care of guest luggage in a far more comprehensive manner.

There were these package deals that not only covered airfare and rooms but also included the complimentary pick-up and delivery of guest luggage to and from the airport. Unfortunately, that option was eliminated after 9/11.

When the policy was still in place, a woman who had ordered the package and was in the process of checking out suddenly called down to the front desk to frantically ask if her luggage had already been sent to the airport. Indeed, it had.

The poor woman was in her pajamas and had forgotten to lay out a change of clothes while packing. Rather than opt for the last-minute expense of a new outfit, she made instead like an eccentric rich person and headed to McCarren International Airport in her nightgown.

One would hope that she was able to change before getting onto the airplane. Then again, this being Vegas, any onlooker might simply have assumed that the poor lady had lost her shirt at the casinos.

Sounding the Alarm

I had a guest staying at our hotel that I was very familiar with. He had stayed with us several times, and before that, he'd stayed numerous times at another hotel that I'd worked at. It was a common thing for us to joke back and forth like friends. One day, the alarm in our hotel went off. It had been going off frequently as of late, so my co-worker and I thought nothing of it, knowing the alarm would be traced to the source by security.

My guest, however, didn't know this, and came running into the lobby towards the concierge desk. "Should I be concerned?" he asked breathlessly, still huffing and puffing from his run.

"Concerned about what?" I asked, giving him one of my playful grins. "The fire alarm," he replied. I said, "Well, do you see me running?" He raised an eyebrow and chuckled, replying, "No, I guess not."

"Don't worry about it. The alarm has been going off for a few days pretty frequently. I'll definitely let you know if there's anything to be worried about, though," I said. He thanked me and left the lobby. About ten minutes later, the alarm was still going off, and he returned to the lobby. After walking over to the concierge desk again, he gave me a funny look.

"Something wrong?" I asked. He shook his head. "No. I was just checking to see if you were running yet."

We shared a laugh, but the next moment the fire alarm was shut off. The guests were notified that the alarm was false, but as my guest left the lobby, he kept glancing back insecurely, as if I were going to run when he wasn't looking!

Done Like Dinner

At one point, gentlemen in Las Vegas were required to wear a dinner jacket, tie and socks to gain entry into fine dining establishments. No Bermuda shorts or bare-ankle loafers were allowed. During this bygone era, a particular guest had forgotten to bring his socks. It was late, and there were no shops open so that the man could purchase what he needed. He came to the concierge desk for advice. We talked for a minute, and I let him know that pretty much everything was closed.

"You could always coat your ankles with shoe polish," I joked. He didn't laugh or say anything in response, so I figured he just didn't think my joke was that funny. The very next afternoon, the same guest approached me at the concierge desk again.

"Okay," he said, "so how do I get the shoe polish off? My wife won't let me join her at the pool until I get it cleaned up." I immediately looked down at the man's ankles to see the dark black polish that he'd used. I couldn't believe it! The man had obviously failed to realize that I was joking and had shoe polished his ankles the night before to get into our five-star steakhouse.

From that point on, I was very careful to make sure my guests knew when I was joking!

Minding the Mangos

When I first started to work as a concierge, I came across a mango sitting on the ground in front of my desk. I went to my manager and said, "Look what I found." The manager said, "Oh, a mango." I chuckled a bit and said, "Is it yours?" When she told me no, I threw it in the trash. A little while later, my manager asked me what I did with the mango.

I said, "I threw it away." Shaking her head, she said, "No. You have to turn it into the Lost and Found department." I stood there for a moment, waiting for her to laugh, but it became apparent that she wasn't joking. "Are you serious?" I asked.

"Very serious," she replied. "Once, we had a security officer who picked up a penny and put it into his pocket. Because he didn't turn it in, and it happened to be some guest's lucky penny, he got suspended."

I suspected that my manager was playing a joke on me; after all, I was the rookie. Still, I went and called security. I said, "I found a mango. Should I turn it into you guys?" There was a pause on the line before the man on duty asked me if I was crazy. I laughed, hung up, and forgot about it.

The very next day, my manager approached me. "What did you do with the mango? Did you turn it into security?" she asked. "No," I said. "I called and they asked me if I was crazy."

"Well we had a guest come by looking for a mango," she said. I was thinking, *you're not serious.* "Where was the mango from?" she asked. I shook my head and replied, "There was a Venezuela sticker on it." She looked relieved and replied, "Oh. Well that's not it, then. Our customer was looking for a mango that was grown in the US."

To this day, I have no idea whether my manger was pulling my leg, but I always make sure I turn everything into Lost and Found!

Don't Mess with Grandma

An older woman was checking in, and it was clear from the moment I laid eyes on her that she wasn't a happy camper. She proceeded to let me know that her flight had been delayed, her luggage was temporarily lost, and her taxi cab driver had decided to take the 'scenic route.' I got the distinct impression that the woman felt as if this was all my fault, and she was certainly looking at me and talking to me as if that was true.

She was in town to participate in a poker tournament, and so I helped her go through her troubles one-by-one. For the ones I couldn't do anything about (the driver of the cab, the flight delay), I just listened and expressed my own chagrin as she gave me details. Little by little, this angry tiger turned into a purring kitten as she got all of those irritations off her chest. We got her checked into her room, and I personally escorted her to the lounge where the poker tournament would take place.

As I was turning to go, the woman – who was old enough to be my grandma – put her hand on my arm and said, "Oh come on. You're not going to stay and have a drink?" Of course, I couldn't because I was on duty. Instead, I said, "I can't right now, but after your day, you deserve to drink one for you and me both!"

Tickets for Twenty Italians

When I first began working as a concierge, I helped a lot of big Italian high-rollers. There were all sorts of transportation requests to see to. One night, I looked up from my desk to see 20 Italian men approaching the desk. They wanted to book flights back home to Italy; all 20 at one time. With the online system, you could only book 10 flights at a time, so I booked those with the intention of booking the other 10 immediately.

Unfortunately, when I pressed the back button, the time and date switched and I didn't realize it. So, I had 10 of my Italians booked but the other 10 booked for some time in the future. Of course, when they went to the airport, 10 had the flight while the other 10 didn't. I was off for the next two days, and rather than going to the concierge on duty, they waited for me to come back to work.

They approached my desk again and showed me the receipt for the flight tickets. That's when I noticed it had been the wrong date. Oh no! I thought. These were very important guests and I had messed their flights up. I called the airline only to be told that they could have reimbursed the guest had it only been 24 hours. It had been more than two days! Refusing to refund the money, the airline gave the men a credit for the next year.

The leader of the group completely lost it. He was saying all sorts of things that his friend was translating for me. There were numerous expletives and he threatened me that he'd never use my concierge service again. Hey... sometimes you win, sometimes you lose, and sometimes you just 'plane' mess up!

Serious Steam

Naughty Bits

One of the funniest things about people in Las Vegas is that they're less inhibited. They come to Vegas to have an amazing time and when they arrive, their insecurities seem to go out the door! Sometimes, they try to get the concierge to help them get certain items, or do certain things. This can often be fun and hilarious, but sometimes, a concierge has to lay down the law. As you'll see from the following stories, things can really get steamy in Las Vegas.

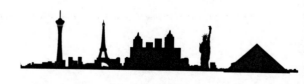

Live Nude Ladies

A group of women who would be staying with us wanted to celebrate their friend's bachelorette party a 'special' way. Rather than going to the strip club to get an eyeful of the male dancers, this group of 12 wanted to get on stage and dance for their friend – no holds barred! Unfortunately, the strip clubs in Las Vegas are very strict when it comes to their dancers and there are rules and regulations for miles.

When I told the girls it wouldn't be possible, they wouldn't be dissuaded. "There must be one strip club where we can give it a try," they pleaded. Without much hope, I called around to nearly every strip club in Vegas and asked if it would be possible. None of the clubs would have anything to do with it until I got in touch with an owner who was a very good friend of mine. He said, "The condition for your girls to dance is that they have to audition. Also, even if they do make it, they can only spend two songs on stage." With no experience dancing, I was sure these girls were in for disappointment.

With a plan in mind, I had the girls take classes a few different times at a great little place on the Strip. Even with that, only 6 of the girls were allowed to go on stage. The girls were so excited to be able to do this for their friend, but on dance night, 2 of the girls chickened out at the last minute. Still, the other 4 went up there and gave it all they had. They pulled the bachelorette on stage, embarrassed and giggling, and tied her to the chair and danced their two songs. They really enjoyed themselves and had a great time.

The hilarious thing was that later, I got a call from the owner of the club who said, "Hey, if you have requests like that in the future, please let me know. We took in more money during the girls' dance than we did with our professionals all night long!" I loved the fact that I was able to pull this off for them. When the girls were leaving, they were so grateful to me, and it was really one of those moments where I was truly rewarded for doing the job I loved. Oh, and the 2 girls who had chickened out at the last moment had to leave the hotel wearing chicken feathers.

With a bit of teasing, I offered the girls a dance of my own, but they declined. They might have had the courage to dance nude on stage and wear chicken feathers, but I guess everyone has their limits!

Show and Tell

During a time when an important, high-betting guest was staying at our hotel, a bellman approached me with a request. Immediately, I could tell it wasn't a standard request, based on the bellman's amused smirk and swagger. Referring to our important guest, he said, "We have a very important issue with Dave... well actually, Dave's girlfriend."

Enjoying the thought of building the sensation, the bellman continued, "It seems that she needs a" – he gestured a little, fingers pointing toward his chest – "a ring." I cocked my head to the side. "A ring?" I asked. The bellman exhaled and then looked around conspiratorially before leaning toward me and whispering, "A nipple ring!"

You've got to be kidding me, I thought. Knowing that Dave and his entourage were out near the pool, I went in that direction, trying very hard to look like I handled this sort of problem all the time. The 112-degree weather felt more like 150, and by the time I'd reached the group, bullets of sweat were forming under my black, three-piece suit. As I arrived at the cabana, a young girl came bouncing up to me.

"Hi. I'm Vanessa. Listen, thanks so much. I'm in trouble." She then– without any hesitation or reservation at all –yanks down her top, revealing both breasts. "My piercing came out," Vanessa added. At this point I am struggling to keep my shock from twisting my face into a mask of disbelief, and to keep my eyeballs in their sockets. She gave me a pitiful look. "I think the ball fell off and it won't stay in."

I nodded slowly. "Okay." I knew a little bit about piercing, so I asked what gauge ring she needed, hoping to quickly make my escape. "I don't know." She frowned, and then suddenly, she pulled the piercing out of the nipple and thrusts it towards me. "Here. Maybe you can tell me."

Pulling out the tiny notebook I kept in my pocket, I smiled, and held it out to her. She placed the little ring on the notebook and bounced back to the group to enjoy the pool some more. With a sigh, I went off to find the girl a new nipple ring. After coating the piece of jewelry in a generous helping of Lysol and storing it in a zippered bag, I set off. About 30 to 40 minutes later, I returned victorious, a brand new nipple ring in hand. I made the journey back out to the cabana, where Vanessa approached me with a grin.

After handing over the jewelry, I prepared to leave, but was stopped when Vanessa asked if I could help her insert the jewelry. Politely, I said, "I'm afraid I can't do that... legal purposes, you know. I would be happy to take you to a professional." She was already shaking her head. "No, but maybe you have a pair of pliers?" Inwardly and involuntarily, I winced. "I'm afraid not. We would be liable for any damages." My eyes darted side to side, taking in the crowd of people surrounding us, enjoying the heat and the pool.

By this time, I didn't think I could become any more uncomfortable with both the topic we were discussing and the sweltering heat. Just as I was prepared to say my goodbyes and leave Vanessa with the task of figuring out how to jam the nipple ring into her flesh by herself, she leans forward a few inches and says, "So, I was thinking of getting this awesome genital piercing..."

Special Delivery

One of our guests was turning twenty-one and in advance of her arrival in Las Vegas for the big birthday celebration, the girl's wealthy mother wanted to make special arrangements.

The mom went ahead and FedEx-ed some gifts to the concierge desk, asking that they be placed in the room ahead of her daughter's check-in. When the shipment arrived, I was surprised to discover that it was nothing but frilly lingerie and sex toys. Sex toys!

Mom and daughter were both from Los Angeles, a town where it is not unusual for rich parents to give young daughters the gift of breast augmentation surgery. Still, it felt decidedly odd to be lining up the daughter for a debauched stay with items provided by mom.

Judging by the variety of young men I saw the daughter with during her stay, mom's plan worked. For better... or worse.

Good Vibrations

I had a guest who was celebrating her 50th birthday in Vegas, and she apparently wanted to make it really special. She gave me five-hundred dollars, and told me to spend the money in an 'adult' store, and put the goods in her room. She was giggling and everything!

Oh my god, I thought. You can buy a lot of stuff for five-hundred dollars! I was trying to determine what I should buy for her. I was thinking I could get some lotions, edible panties, chocolate novelties... but I would still have so much money left over. I was discussing it with a few members of my staff, who just adored the woman and the fact that she'd left this task to me. They thought it was absolutely hilarious.

Suddenly, I had a thought. "You know," I said to my staff members, "you guys are so perverted," – I joked – "that I think you should do the shopping!" Not surprisingly, they jumped at the opportunity. It was like Christmas for them. A few hours later, after finishing some other errands, I returned to my desk to find that the entire surface of it was covered in items that were buzzing, twirling and rotating. There were lotions, oils, videos, and numerous other items.

I was standing there looking at the mini sex shop that was my desk when my boss walked into the office. Accustomed to the ways of Vegas, my easy-going boss took a long look at my desk, looked back up at me and said, "What happens at the concierge desk stays at the concierge desk." With his hands in the air, he walked out of my office, smiling, without ever asking about the items! My colleagues and I decorated the woman's room with all of the paraphernalia, and she was thrilled.

Indecent Exposure

I'll never forget a particular bachelorette party at our hotel. It was in full swing, and with a huge lineup of bridesmaids, there was a lot to do. As I was scrambling around to make sure everything was perfect, a bridesmaid came down to the concierge desk carrying a big box. She was absolutely giddy, and I was glad the group was having a good time. She asked if I could unpack the item, blow it up and bring it upstairs.

I took the thing out and quickly realized there was no way I was going to be able to blow it up by myself, so I recruited a couple of guys from maintenance to help inflate it. They were happy to oblige, and as they were blowing it up, I made a few phone calls and wrote down a few things that I still had to do for the bachelorette party. I was a little flustered because I was so busy, so I guess I was in my own little world.

When one of the maintenance men cleared his throat, I glanced up to see him standing next to an 8-foot penis. He only turned slightly red when I couldn't help but cackle. However, both maintenance men left the job of carrying this very realistic-looking male appendage through the hotel lobby and guest areas to me. It's pretty safe to say they got the last laugh.

Party Girls

I was a few weeks into my first Las Vegas concierge job, and I got a rather unusual call from one of the penthouse suites. "Could you send up some ladies?" the bachelor asked. "Nothing illegal, of course. We just need some ladies to make our party more interesting."

I politely told my guest that I couldn't help him – it was against our policy, regardless of how tame the expectations are. Apparently, he was a believer in the theory that everything is possible if you throw enough money around. He called back a few minutes later to lay out his request in greater detail.

"I'll pay you $1,000 for each woman you can get up here, and I'll pay the women $1,000 each as well. I just want them to hang out, maybe take their tops off." I told the young man that I was sorry, but that there was no way I'd be able to help him. In fact, even if I'd wanted to help him, I didn't even know six girls in town yet. About an hour later, I saw a few beautiful girls making their way to the bank of hotel elevators and disappearing. A moment later, there was a couple more. The girls disappeared for a few hours before leaving.

I have no idea where the man found these women, but I know they were paid well. "Are you kidding me?" One of my friends asked when I told her about the man's request. "I would have totally gone and spent a few hours hanging out at a party for $1,000." I laughed and said, "Maybe so, but then you'd have had to let me sleep on your couch because I'd have been out of a job!"

Basic Instinct

Late one evening, a call came in to the concierge desk from a male guest.

"I'd like to speak to a male concierge, please," the man insisted. When I explained that I was the only concierge on duty at that hour and would be happy to assist with whatever it was that he needed, he reiterated his request. "No, it has to be a man!"

The only staff member on call at that time who fit the bill was my manager. I felt bad about having to bother him, but the guest was insistent. When I summoned my manager, somewhat apologetically, he rolled his eyes. "I would be willing to bet this call has something to do with female companionship," he predicted.

Sure enough, the manager was soon informing the guest a referral to a lady of the evening was not something that could be provided by concierge services. Then again, it could have been worse. The guest could have asked how much I would charge to head up to the room in a non-concierge capacity.

Loss of Innocence

Occasionally, Las Vegas concierges have to 'learn the hard way.' I was the new kid on the block when a guest approached me. She was giggling a little, but managed to ask where the closest chicken ranch was. Since I wasn't from the US, I had no idea where one might be, but I told her I'd check and get back to her. I did a Google search locally for 'chicken ranch' but came up with nothing.

When I went into the back room, a few of my colleagues were there. I thought about asking them for help, but decided I would be embarrassed for not having found it myself. Rolling my eyes at myself, I began to search through our reference materials in hopes of finding information about a chicken ranch nearby.

After a few minutes, one of my colleagues noticed my frantic searching and said, "What in the world are you looking for?" I said, "I'm trying to find the nearest chicken ranch for a guest."

He looked at me for a moment and then burst out laughing. "What?" I asked. After taking a second to catch his breath, he said, "A chicken ranch is a brothel... a whore house," he said. "We can't help the guests look for those." I was so purely embarrassed just then, I think I could have fallen over in the floor, but I managed to stay on my feet.

"Oh," I said. I got back with the guest and let her know that it was against our policy to give out that sort of information. She took it well, but my colleagues teased me for so long. They kept telling me it was a shame that I had to lose my innocence like that, and eventually I just said, "I guess it was bound to happen in this town sooner or later!"

A New Day

One of the funniest things I experienced as a concierge involves a frumpy but very animated middle-aged woman from western Canada. She was a professional who was entertaining clients. "Wouldn't you know it," she said to me, "my client's wife wants to see Celine Dion in concert." It just so happened that this woman couldn't stand Celine Dion.

"It's a wonderful show," I said. "It's really one of the best I've seen." So, I was left with the task of getting tickets to this wildly popular show. Just by luck, I was able to get the client couple and their chaperone up with phenomenal seats: third row, center.

As they left for the concert, I couldn't help thinking how excited the couple looked, while the chaperone appeared to be wishing she were anywhere else. Imagine my surprise when after the show, the chaperone couldn't stop raving about Celine Dion. She'd purchased a shirt, a souvenir CD, and the whole nine yards. By the time she and her clients left, she'd managed to see the Celine Dion show twice more, convinced it was one of the finest concerts she'd ever experienced. It was what I'd call a 'titanic' turnaround!

Counting Their Cards

Crimes and Misdemeanors

Occasionally, a concierge is asked to do something illegal or unethical. Of course, they will not do anything illegal for a guest, but letting the guest know that can sometimes be difficult. In fact, these situations can often be extremely uncomfortable, and even funny at times. As you'll see from the following stories, guests often think that a concierge can literally get them anything they want!

Party Supplies

A hotel guest approached me and inquired about night clubs. He and I talked for a little while about DJ's, and the different types of clubs. Before he left, he wrote something on a piece of paper and handed it to me. "I need a favor," he said. "My friends and I are planning to hit some of the top Vegas clubs tonight. That's the combination to my hotel room safe, and here's three-hundred dollars. Let's just say we want to party... all night."

Now, my first thought was that the man wanted me to make sure there was a car available to him. When the man left, I got to thinking and wondered why he'd given me the combination to his room safe. Maybe he thought I would need more than three-hundred dollars? Puzzled, I told my colleague about it, and he got a 'knowing' look on his face.

"What?" I asked. "He wants you to score him some drugs," my colleague said. "The money is to pay for them, and he wants you to put them in his hotel room safe."

Oh no! I thought. How could I have possibly misunderstood that? And now the man thinks I'm going to deliver drugs to his hotel room. "Oh my gosh," I said to my colleague. "I had no idea." Embarrassed and horrified at the thought of going out on the Strip to try and score recreational drugs, I had to track down the guest and give back his money.

"I'm sorry, sir," I said. "I misunderstood you. I can make arrangements for your night but I can't help you with the other thing you need." The guest wasn't fazed as he accepted the money back. He shrugged. "That's okay," he said. "I actually just got it taken care of," and he gestured to his phone. I made my escape quickly before he revealed anything else I really didn't want to know.

204

Rx Marks the Spot

A Hawaiian-shirted guest came up to the concierge desk one day with a question. He shifted his weight from one foot to the other a few times, and then he said, "I have a question for you. It's going to be kind of weird." I thought, well, I'm good with weird. "I need some marijuana," he said.

"Oh," I said. "That kind of weird. I'm sorry but I can't help you with that." The man shook his head. "It's not what you think. I actually have a prescription for medical marijuana because I have glaucoma." I had the feeling that the guest had been testing me before, and so I pretended to think about it for a moment.

"I apologize, but I don't think there's any place in Las Vegas that would fill a prescription for medical marijuana," I said. The man frowned and said, "Is there nothing you can think of?"

I finally ended up telling the man that there was a Walgreens just up the street and that I could give him the phone number and directions. Seeing that he wasn't going to get anywhere with me, the guest told me that he'd work it out himself and thanked me.

Several hours later, I spotted the same guest enjoying himself by the pool with a couple of friends, and I wondered if he'd found a 'pharmacist' for his marijuana or not. Judging by the amount of room service he ordered later, I'd be willing to bet that he did.

A Coded Message

One of the things I'll never get used to as a concierge is when people come up to me and ask for drugs. I am a laid-back, outgoing person, and I think this is the reason people feel I should be able to help them out with those kinds of requests. The truth is, I know absolutely nothing about drugs. Even when I was a high school teacher, my students had to explain what crack was.

Once, a guy came up to the desk and he asked me, "Do you know TINA? Is TINA in town?" I stood there a moment and thought. Tina Turner hadn't been to Vegas in some time, and I couldn't recall any other celebrity named Tina. Come on, I thought to myself, think. Tina... Tina. Finally, I admitted to the man that I wasn't sure, and asked him who Tina was. He simply said, "Never mind, that's okay."

I felt really bad that I wasn't able to help this guest, but as I was relating the story to my co-worker, he said, "TINA means drugs. He was asking you to help him get some drugs, or give him information about where to get them here." I was completely floored, and found the lyrics of a Tina Turner song coming to mind... What does logic have to do with it?

An Uncomfortable Conversation

One particular afternoon, a middle-aged Kentucky man asked for my help in purchasing a gift for his girlfriend.

"I want to buy her something feminine and pretty," he said. "Maybe some lingerie or pajamas." I nodded and said, "That's a great idea. There are a number of fabulous shops nearby where you could find a perfect gift."

The man nodded and said, "Well what kind of lingerie do you think is the best?" I thought for a moment and replied that he should probably find something that reminded him of his girlfriend; something that he thought she would like. He then said, "Well what brand of bra do you think is sexiest?"

At this point, I started to feel uncomfortable, because I thought the man should be worried about what kind of bra his lady friend thought was sexiest, not me. I replied, "I don't know. You should probably think about what she usually wears."

After a moment, the man said. "What is your size? Have you ever worn crotchless panties, because that's something I was thinking about buying for her." At this point, I was really beginning to creeped out by the conversation, and I politely ended the conversation, telling the man that I couldn't help him.

A few weeks later, I heard through the hotel grapevine that a southern gentleman had been busted by police at another property on the Strip after trying to steal women's underwear from a room. The perpetrator turned out to be – that's right – Mr. Kentucky. My instincts were correct all along.

Search and Rescue

Early one Sunday morning, a pair of Scandinavian girls in their 20s rushed into the hotel lobby and came over to the concierge desk, crying hysterically.

Although there was a bit of a language barrier, I was able to eventually discern that they had been up drinking all night and had long ago lost the trail of their male friend, a fellow student. "We need you to please help find Jakob," they implored.

There is a set routine for this scenario, one that begins with calls to security and bell captains, then moves on to major hospitals and the local police station. When all that failed to turn up any leads, the girls insisted on filling out a missing person's report. Even though it was a tad premature to take such drastic action, I decided it might put their minds a little more at ease.

The girls kept frantically sending texts to their friend and calling his cell phone. Finally, with the paperwork completed, they turned dejectedly from the desk and headed for their room.

As they were about to walk through an open elevator door, out popped their friend Jakob. He claimed to have stumbled into a hotel stairwell in a drunken haze and fallen asleep on a landing. I knew for a fact that if that was the case, our security patrols would have found him within hours. Still, I decided to play dumb.

If you ask me, a third and most likely non-Scandinavian young woman was responsible for Jakob's overnight "disappearance."

Longshots

A Time for Miracles

It's a wonderful thing for a concierge to be able to make a dream come true. Whether it's ensuring that a guest has an amazing time, or delivering something the guest would never think possible – these are the moments when a concierge truly feels like they're serving a guest. It can be a privilege, an honor, and very emotional as well!

Getting Away from Gomorrah

The sweetest concierge experience I had occurred toward the end of my career. A female guest and her nine year-old son were here with her husband, who was participating in a convention. She had requested something small from me, and then it seemed like she wanted to vent. She said to me, "I absolutely hate this place. I can't stand it." I was surprised, but could clearly tell that she was seething. "The only reason we're here is because of my husband's convention, and he wanted to turn it into a family vacation. A family vacation in Vegas. This place is a modern age Sodom and Gomorrah."

It was easy to see that she hated Vegas and everything it stood for. I said, "Look, we can make things fun for you. We can turn it around and make sure that you have a really good time."

"Right," she said, sarcastically. "I'm serious," I insisted. "Just let me handle everything."

Because she didn't believe Vegas would ever suffice for a family vacation, I decided to show her how much fun it can actually be. I got tickets for the Hoover Dam, Red Rock Canyon, and Mount Charleston. I also got a few show tickets for a beautiful circus show that I thought they'd both love. Then, for the last night, I got a licensed and bonded babysitter and provided the little boy with a bunch of great in-room movies so that the mother and father could go out and enjoy a nice dinner and a bottle of champagne.

When the guests were checking out, the woman approached me and said, "Thank you so much! I cannot believe how much I love this place. You proved me completely wrong, and I think I had the best time of my life here."

The couple and their son came back every year after that for vacation, and I served them until I retired.

Catching the Fever

We help a fair share of guests find the right costume for Halloween or masquerade parties throughout the year. I remember one guy who was due at a costume party later in the evening, and he came to me for help. He had no idea which costume he should choose. I ended up getting him the John Travolta outfit from Saturday Night Fever. My guest looked fabulous in his costume, and he knew it.

He came sauntering into the lobby once he'd transformed into Tony Manero, and he swept me off my feet! He danced me all around the lobby, doing all the John Travolta moves. It was hilarious – guests were pausing to watch and giggle. I picked the wrong costume, I thought. I mean, I love dancing, but...

His attitude was just great. He acted as if he owned the place, and it was so comical to behold. We stopped dancing just as some of the guests began to snap pictures of the two of us. He had such a great time that he came back every year, and he'd say, "I need my John Travolta costume and you'd better be ready to dance!"

So every year, Mr. Travolta and I jig around the lobby while the guests laugh and take pictures. I can't help but form a picture in my mind of an 80-year old me dancing with a cane-bearing John Travolta – but it's memories like this that make the job wonderful!

In a Fix

One morning, a bride-to-be walked up to the concierge desk in her full wedding day attire. She was wearing a gorgeous dress, the shoes, her hair was immaculate – but she was crying! "What's the matter?" I asked. Apparently, she'd sent her dress out a few weeks earlier to be altered, and it had come back to the hotel with an anti-theft device attached to the skirt. Somehow, she'd failed to notice this until the very last minute.

There were three things that made this situation much worse. The first was that the dress was a fitted dress and the fabric was very sleek, so there was no way to hide the device in the folds of the gown. The second was that it was one of those anti-theft capsules that spilled ink all over the garment if it was broken, so there was no strong-arming it. The third was that the bride-to-be's entire family (aunts, cousins, sisters) were standing in the lobby, nervously whispering back and forth to each other.

Since I worked as a costume creator for a theater prior to my concierge career, I pulled on that experience and I called down to housekeeping for a sewing kit. The whole time I was waiting for it, I was thinking, *oh man. What the hell am I going to do?* When the kit arrived, I saw that I had a few spools of thread, some scissors, and a needle to work with – no miracle anti-theft-capsule-removing tool, unfortunately.

In a few minutes, I was down on my knees in front of the bride-to-be, who was still distraught. I smiled up at her, trying to look calm even though I was in a panic. I was thinking, *what if I ruin this gown? How much is it going to cost me? Not to mention that it would ruin this woman's entire wedding day!* Taking a deep breath,

I started cutting the fabric near the anti-theft device. I could hear gasps behind me, and one of the aunties whispered, "Oh dear lord, he's cutting the dress."

With that, the room broke out into whispers: "He's cutting the dress, he's cutting the dress," and it was like I could hear the panic flowing through the bride. Although I'm fairly confident about my seamstress skills, I really started to second-guess myself. Still, I kept going until I had the device out of the dress. At that point, I stole some fabric from the hemline so I could patch up the spot where I'd operated. My boss then walked into the room and absorbed the situation. Kneeling down beside me for a moment, he whispered, "Are you sure you know what you're doing?"

I felt like having him wipe the sweat from my upper lip and hand me the needle, just like a good nurse would do, but instead, I just nodded. In a few more minutes, I had the hole patched up perfectly. Without seriously close inspection, you could never tell it had been cut in the first place. The bride was thrilled, and after the wedding, they ordered me flowers and showered me in thanks. A few weeks later, I was voted Hotel Employee of the Month, and I still believe it was directly related to my mad skills with a needle and thread.

Runaway Dress

Many Las Vegas brides-to-be arrive ahead of their wedding dresses, planning to either shop for one in Las Vegas or take receipt of the gown after they have arrived. I had this one couple who checked in and were scheduled to get married a few days after their arrival, on a Sunday. The bride's wedding dress arrived the day before, on a Saturday. However, the couple were out all day and didn't return to their room until late Saturday night.

When she opened the package, she found a dress that was the wrong color, wrong style, and the wrong size. The company had somehow sent her another woman's bridal gown. Of course, it was now in the middle of the night, and there was no way to order another gown. She came to me absolutely distraught. They were going to get married in the morning and the bride had no wedding dress.

I called every single wedding boutique I could find in the phone book, but none of them were open. A colleague of mine just happened to be very good friends with the owner of a dress shop, and so we called him at nearly midnight. He came out and opened up his shop, and we took the guest there and had her fitted for a new dress. We were so grateful to the shop owner, and the bride-to-be was thrilled with her new dress, and relieved to have something to wear to her wedding. She got a full refund from the store that had shipped her the wrong dress, which ended up covering the cost of the new dress, as well as a large chunk of her Hawaiian honeymoon!

Saturday Night Special

An important part of the concierge job description is wrangling last-minute show and concert tickets for guests.

The pinnacle for me was a young Hungarian couple that came to Las Vegas wanting to see Celine Dion on one of the last weekends of her Caesar's Palace contract, without prior reservations. Mission impossible, basically.

Still, I was determined to try and make it happen for them. With only a day or so to work with, I pleaded my case all the way up to the top of the Caesar's Palace food chain, explaining how much a pair of tickets would mean to my European guests. Understandably, there was nothing they could do.

Late the next afternoon, my Blackberry buzzed with an email notification that Caesar's had received a last-minute cancellation for Dion's Saturday show. The Hungarian couple could not believe their good fortune and neither could I. It was almost as fateful as those moments in Titanic played out to Dion's number one ballad "My Heart Will Go On."

Rope-a-Dope

Heavyweight boxing matches are always a big deal in Las Vegas. A unique crowd and atmosphere invades the Strip whenever a title bout is at hand. One weekend, a high-roller approached the concierge desk at 7:15pm and asked for ringside seats to the event that was scheduled to happen at 8pm!

Now, usually, these fights are completely sold out months in advance, and it was no different for this one. This was one of those moments when the numbers in a concierge's little black book can be immeasurably helpful. I dialed the cell phone number of the owner of a major ticket brokering firm on the Strip and he quickly answered. It turns out that he was at the location where the fight would take place, and he had a few tickets on him.

I quickly explained the situation, and was able to get my guest two tickets. They weren't quite ringside, but the guest was still happy. Or, at least he was happy enough to pay $6,000 per ticket! He had a great time at the event, and thanked me numerous times for getting the tickets. Sometimes, concierges will try their best and still won't be able to fulfill a guest's request, but occasionally, even a concierge gets a great knock-out under their belt!

Mediterranean Mix-Up

Part of the job of a concierge is to help out current and former desk colleagues in their time of need. One day, a former colleague of mine called me from her home in the Philippines. She knew that I was from Italy, and remembered that one of my cousins was an Italian police officer. Her brother had been working on a cruise ship, and had been arrested when the ship docked at an Italian port.

Her family was very worried, and no one spoke the language, so they were having a very difficult time figuring out what to do or getting any details. I told her that I'd give my cousin a call, and we'd see what we could find out. When I got in touch with my cousin, I explained the problem. He was able to guide my ex-colleague through the arcane Italian process of getting the brother released.

It had all turned out to be a big misunderstanding; the Italian authorities thought the man was someone he wasn't, and they apologized when they released him. As you can imagine, the family was so relieved, and my ex-colleague thanked me profusely for helping. It was a situation where I was able to help a fellow concierge, as well as the poor family who couldn't get any information.

Monkey Business

A group of businessmen was staying at the hotel for a conference. They wanted to do a short skit that involved a purple gorilla suit. This request was made on the day of the event, so we were under a lot of pressure to find something quickly. I began calling costume stores immediately, and couldn't find a purple gorilla suit to save my life! I finally found a shop that had a pink gorilla suit, and we decided we'd get that one and dye it purple for the skit.

So, we ran out and got the purple dye and we put it into a lined trash can and put the gorilla suit in. We stirred and stirred, and the suit only seemed to soak up a small amount of the dye. It wasn't really purple, and it wasn't really pink; it was somewhere in the middle. We decided it would have to work, because we were quickly running out of time. We hung the costume out in the sun, knowing that it would dry very quickly with the sweltering Vegas heat.

The problem was, we'd been so worried about finding a suit in the right color that we didn't think too much about the size of the person who would be wearing it! When it came time to suit him up, he had to hunch over to get in it. He sucked in and tried to make himself compact while we yanked and yanked on the zipper. Guests who were passing by must have thought we were engaging in some form of medieval torture on this poor guy!

The funniest thing is that for the skit, the poor guy had to hunch over while he ran because the costume was too small! He ended up playing the perfect gorilla because of this little glitch, but I imagine he was pretty sore the next day.

Christmas in July

I got a call from a man one day – we'll call him Peter – and Peter said to me, "I have to tell you a little story so you'll understand my request. When I was ten years old..." And I thought, oh dear, this is going to be a long story. He continued, "That summer, my best friend's mom made him this snowman doll. Now, boys that age aren't supposed to like those kinds of things but I really thought the doll was super-cool. He took it to his father's with him that summer, to remind him of home. When I went to summer camp the next summer, his mom sent the doll so that I'd have something to remind me of my friend.

Over the years, it became a bit of a joke between us. We'd send it to each other every single summer, and even if we didn't talk much that year, it became a way for us to keep in touch. Well, for some reason, my friend hasn't sent me the snowman doll in about three years, but I've had his mother go into his house and 'steal' the doll, and I want to send it to him. He's in Vegas right now, and I can't be there, but I'd like to surprise him with the doll."

I thought the story was charming, and I told him we could definitely do that. So, he sent me the doll, and he had a special request. It was his friend's birthday, and I called Peter when the doll arrived. He said, "Where's John at right now?" I said, "He's out by the pool." So, he asked if I could take the doll out by the pool and sing Happy Birthday to John. I chuckled a little and then shrugged. It's not the worst thing I've been asked to do.

So, I took the snowman doll out by the pool and put on a little puppet act, singing Happy Birthday to John. No doubt his friends wondered what in the world was going on, but when John saw the snowman doll, he was over the moon. "I can't believe this," he said. "My friend hasn't sent me that doll in three years, and I kind of thought we were drifting. That's incredible." I explained to him that he was the one who had the doll, and that his mother had been a co-conspirator and had helped us get the doll. He couldn't believe it. Neither could Peter when I explained that John had thought he'd had the doll all this time.

It was super-funny, and I told John that he should probably call Peter and catch up. He promised he would, and I was happy to have helped the friends reconnect after the misunderstanding.

A Priceless Proposal

I was enlisted for help by a guy who wanted to propose to his girl-friend. The heart does not acknowledge price tags, and the guy had just $100 to make it happen. Of course, like most guys, he wanted it to be special for his special lady. I rolled the number around in my head a bit, and then nervously asked the man if he already had the ring. Thank goodness, it was a yes! After a bit of thinking, I set to work on a plan using the old traditional saying, 'something old, something new, something borrowed, something blue.'

We had a car rental at our office so I went to the agent and told the story, asking whether she could provide a discount on a car, and if she could possibly provide a blue car. She pulled through, charging only $35. With that out of the way, I called another hotel in Las Vegas and spoke to the chef, again telling the story and asking if a set menu could be created for $60 or less, including the tip. So a special menu was created for the couple; a dish, dessert, and coffee for the two.

I spent a fair amount of time coaching our guy about what he should do and what he should say. So, on the night of the proposal, they took the car to the restaurant, had a delicious meal, and then they took a walk around the lake. The guy told his girl the story of how they met during their walk, and then they returned to the car. That's where he said, "This car is blue, and it's borrowed." He pulled out the ring and continued, "This ring is new, and I want to grow old with you."

Of course, the girl was in tears and said she would marry the guy. Unfortunately, during my planning, I had completely forgotten about filling up the gas tank in the rental car before returning it. The girl ended up paying for the gas. Perhaps it was a perfect beginning lesson about the give and take of love!

Sound and Fury

I got a panicked call from a man completely across the country. "My wife is on her way there. I arranged everything and packed everything for her. But I completely forgot something of terrible importance. It's a CD with thunder effects for a private concert performance my wife is scheduled to be part of!"

I calmed the caller down and got his phone number, then told him I'd see what I could do. It was Sunday morning, so there were no audio or video shops open at that point. However, I had theater experience and had a few contacts. So I called up one of my friends who just so happened to be working on a local stage show version of Mamma Mia. I said, "I have a huge emergency," and I explained the situation.

He was wonderful, and before long I had a CD with 35 different thunder sound effects. I left a little note on the CD and placed it in the guest's room. It said, "By now you may or may not have figured out that you've forgotten your sound effects CD. Here is one with plenty of thunder effects. I hope it's useful."

The woman was absolutely thrilled! She said these effects were better than the ones that she would have brought herself. Later that night, the concert symphony went off without a hitch and a thank you bouquet of yellow roses adorned my desk the next day.

Today, whenever people ask me what I can do for guests, I sometimes trot out the line, "Thunder and lightning, if necessary."

A Bra Brouhaha

It was New Year's Eve, and a particular woman staying in our hotel had gone out and purchased a very expensive designer dress. She was so excited about getting all dolled up and looking her best at the stroke of midnight. At about 10pm on December 31st, the woman calls my desk in a panic. She'd purchased a specific bra to wear under her designer dress, and she couldn't find it anywhere. She had only a few minutes before she had to leave for her party.

"Are there any stores open still?" she asked breathlessly. "At this hour," I replied, "none of them are going to have that kind of specialized merchandise. The major department stores and women's boutiques close at 9pm."

I felt horrible for this woman, because a bra was going to ruin her whole night. She began explaining the kind she needed. "Oh darn. It's one of those criss-cross ones with removable straps. I can't believe this," she said, disappointed.

"Oh, I know exactly what you're taking about," I said. "I wear the same kind."

"Wait," she said. "Are you wearing it now?" Chuckling, I replied, "As a matter of fact, I am."

She immediately jumped on the opportunity, asking what cup size I wore and if she could borrow the bra. Of course, in a strange twist of fate, it was the exact same size as mine. In a matter of minutes, the distressed guest was dressed, complete with bra, and I went the rest of my shift bra-less. All in the name of service!

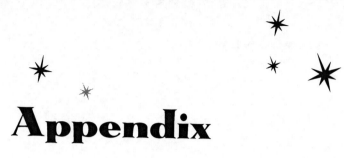

Appendix

You Want WHAT???

What Does
a Las Vegas Concierge Do?

A concierge is defined as someone who attends to the wishes of hotel guests. In Las Vegas, those wishes are numerous and each is as different and diverse as the guests themselves. The term 'concierge' is all-encompassing. The people who hold this title help with everything from celebrations and proposals to shows, dinners, clothing and just about anything else you could think of.

Of course, they serve guests and attempt to make those guests' stays as lovely and comfortable as possible. A concierge uses discretion and kindness in all situations, and sometimes has to engage in some very quick thinking to pull something off at the last minute. One of the very best things about concierges is that the vast majority of them truly love what they do, and enjoy making guests' wishes come true.

While they would never refer to themselves as 'miracle workers,' most of them have had the pleasure of pulling off a miracle or two for their guests at one point or another. In any case, they are the men and women who serve Las Vegas hotel guests to the very best of their abilities.

◆ ◆ ◆ ◆ ◆ ◆

Each Las Vegas concierge interviewed for the book was asked to give a general overview of this sometimes glamorous profession. What follows are some select answers:

"You have to have the passion to want to be a concierge. Instead of thinking, 'Oh gosh, another stupid request', you have to remember that these requests are what make the job so interesting. Each day on the job brings new guests, new requests and an opportunity to rise to the unexpected challenge of it all."

A concierge always has to think quickly on their feet, they have to improvise a lot. A good concierge gets involved with everything at a hotel. Their office is the whole Strip, not just the lobby. They have to keep an eye on everything that's going on. And I mean everything.

• • •

"A big part of the job is weddings. On the Strip, in Red Rock Canyon, at the Grand Canyon. You name a place in Nevada or Arizona and chances are I've helped organized a wedding there for guests. Although these weddings involve the same things that other weddings do – limousine, photographer, minister, champagne, flowers, wedding dress, tux – the challenge is that we often have to make it all happen in the space of just a few days or even hours."

• • •

"I love being a concierge! I love the magic of it. I have been offered the chance to switch over to hotel operations and management, but I said: "Oh God, no! Why would I want to do that?" Guests walk up to the concierge desk because they want to do something fun and exciting, make something extraordinary happen. They come to you because they want to have a good time, not because the water is leaking in the bathroom, the bill is inaccurate or they just lost $10,000!"

• • •

"The best concierges genuinely make an effort to be kind to people and learn about them and their perspective. My job is to understand what guests want and then help them get it. It's not rocket science.

My friends who are not in the service industry often ask me, "How can you do that? You have people in your face all day long and this and that." To me, the guests are the best part of the job and my rapport with them is crucial. A hotel's features and amenities are important, but what really brings back guests year after year are the staff. Conversely, the tips I remember most are not large cash amounts but rather things like books, personal photos and T-shirts."

◆ ◆ ◆

"A good concierge puts people at ease. He or she is an ambassador of the hotel. Our jobs are really simple – to serve and be kind – with the caveat of being able to figure out what type of guests you are dealing with.

Some guests have very specific needs that they just want taken care of, pronto, while others require more hand holding. They want to feel affection and warmth. They want you to get to know them a little bit, so you can help them figure out what they want."

◆ ◆ ◆

"It is an art to be able to say no without saying no. Concierges must learn to dance around certain situations without sounding judgmental or bitchy. My job is to accommodate guests and make them feel welcome, but at the same time, I am certainly not going to do anything illegal or unethical. However, I never want to make them feel bad for asking.

At the same time, there is a small group of people with whom you just have to lay it down. You have to be very cut and dry – I will do this and this, I cannot do that. It's one of the less fun parts of the job, but it's important to not let people walk all over you. As a concierge, you have to be in control of the conversation and situation at all times."

• • •

"You have to be able to raise yourself to different levels. If a guest is super high-end and only interested in dining at places like Rubochan and Gisagoar, you have to seamlessly put yourself in that frame of mind. And then immediately switch to the point of view of a small town visitor who has been saving up for two years to come to Las Vegas. It's all about being adaptable."

• • •

"Most of the time, guests tell you what they want and all you have to do is give it to them. The hard part is when a request is encumbered by certain rules and regulations. Still, it is part of the job to know how to bend those rules and regulations. That's what a concierge often does. The ability to push the envelope without getting a paper cut is a major plus for anyone sitting at the concierge desk."

About the Author

When Hungarian native Mariann Mohos relocated to Las Vegas to pursue a Masters degree in Business Administration, she never imagined that she would one day also become one of the people who are integral to creating memorable experiences for the millions of guests visiting this spectacular and magical city each year.

For the past four years, Mohos has worked as a concierge at one of the major hotel and casino resorts in Las Vegas, where she has established herself as a trusted part of the concierge community.

Always fascinated by the inner workings of the hospitality industry, she has taken the opportunity to meet people from all walks of life, while still having ample time to pursue her own interests. With a command of four different languages, wide-ranging business experience in Europe and the US, and an outgoing personality, Mohos has found that serving as a concierge comes second nature to her.

Along with her love of Las Vegas, Mohos has an immense passion for learning and adores languages, traveling, the outdoors, and exploring different cultures. In addition to her MBA from the University Of Nevada, Las Vegas, she has degrees in English and Russian studies and Economics. Mohos founded and operated a grassroots marketing company for a number of years prior to beginning her career as a Las Vegas concierge.

Lightning Source UK Ltd.
Milton Keynes UK
UKOW041944091012

200301UK00014B/88/P